RUNNING A SUCCESSFUL VOICEOVER BUSINESS

by Joshua Alexander

For Sweeps, Bren & AJ:
My true loves

ISBN # 9798728574460

REVIEWS

"Joshua Alexander asked me to write a review of his new book, *Running a Successful Voiceover Business*, but I am afraid he won't be happy with it. While reading, it didn't take long to figure out that he has made a big mistake.

If you are a subscriber to Josh's blog, you have come to expect a certain amount of his off-the-wall humor. If you are looking for that here, you might be a little disappointed. That is fine; this is just a different type of book. There is humor, of course. I don't think Josh can write for very long without some humor slipping in, but it will be harder to find.

What you *will* find is a condensation of the tools, tactics, techniques and other words that start with 'T' that he has used to become successful. This is where the obvious mistake happens. The curtain has been pulled aside and the fraud has been exposed. Put bluntly, he is pretending to be an authority on the business side of voice-over when that premise is patently nonsense.

I mean, how smart of a businessperson can he be if he hands the Keys to the Kingdom to his potential competitors? He is essentially telling his readers that if you want to compete with him, these are the steps you need to take. How is that good business?

How can a new voice artist trust business advice from someone who tells them how he got to where he is, what pitfalls to watch out for, and which steps you must not skip? Has he never heard of Colonel Sanders and the Eleven Secret Herbs and Spices? Everyone knows that when you have a formula for success, you don't offer it to the world, knowing that it can be used to compete against you.

Even worse is putting all of this useful info into a form compact enough to keep on hand and reference easily. What he has done is provide the secret recipe and then made it microwavable. What is he thinking? Not exactly evidence of a business mind that you should emulate.

The only totally not self-serving wisdom I can offer is to not trust advice from such a person, with or without a superhero cape. In fact, what a savvy person would do is *not* buy this book and tell all your friends not to read it either.

Now excuse me while I go back to reading, taking notes and planning my domination of the voice-over world while you go back to not knowing how to compete with Josh. Or me."

- Jon Gardner, Voice Talent

"THIS is the book every budding and established voice artist should have within arm's reach for quick reference. Its straightforward, cut-to-the-chase material lays out step by step PRECISELY how Josh has managed to amass financial success in a very crowded and competitive field.

Seriously, it's like discovering the secret of how to solve a Rubik's cube. Joshua opens his toolbox of templates, websites and countless other resources.

The only negative I could find about this book would be the omission of any reference to Michael Bolton.

Basically, "*Running A Successful Voiceover Business*" is the culmination of Josh's years of experience, run through a juicer, compressed through a colander and poured into one satisfying super smoothie of success.

5 + Stars!"

- Scott Burns, Voice Talent · Coach · Demo Producer

"If you can read this book without getting crazy-excited, jumping up and down and running into the nearest acoustically-treated space to record something, well then, perhaps you should instead go read a book about paint drying. But if you have a heartbeat and you enjoy voiceover, Joshua's writing inspires exactly that kind of "let's do this!" excitement. Because Josh really loves voiceover, and I suspect he loves helping people just as much.

This book is chock-full of useful, easy to follow advice, with specific action steps and recommendations to help you move from quite fancying the idea of doing voiceover to, well, running a successful voiceover business. Just like it says on the tin.

Josh also reminds me a bit of Shakespeare – 'why use one word when I could use ten plus a joke?' - so grab your notepad and be ready to focus on gently meandering streams of information interspersed with a healthy dose of humor."

- Sumara Meers, Voice Talent

"In his writing, Joshua Alexander provides a detailed and thorough response to the daunting question: 'How do I get started in voiceover?' Joshua shares important stories and experiences through a light-hearted lens, while also teaching the importance (and the how-to) of building and fostering your own personalized voiceover business.

Insights on industry standards and expectations, client acquisition and relationships, P2Ps, branding, and community resources are among the subjects delved into in this fantastic resource for both beginners and experienced talent looking to up their game."

- Michael Apollo Lira, Voice Talent

"Josh has done it again! He has taken his wealth of marketing and business knowledge and made it a fun, encouraging and informative read! Every time I read one of Josh's books, I come away with new and doable information that I can easily implement into my business. I think my favorite quote from this book is: Success is not an event; Success is a journey. Thanks Josh, for generously sharing your journey with us and providing so much encouragement and inspiration along the way."

- Leigh Lovett Laird, Voice Talent

"Joshua Alexander has again brought us a vital tool to help us obtain success in our business. Through straight, no holds barred talk and practical, actionable steps Josh has provided you tools you can use to catapult your business from first gear to fifth gear! Joshua genuinely wants to see his peers succeed. In this book, he tells you how he does it, and how you can too! Make no mistake, this book does not contain a 'blueprint' or magic recipe to cook up success. Instead, Josh provides us with good advice, understandable philosophies, and explanations of why and what he does and does not do. A professionally written, yet with a hint of cynicism, guide to use as a benchmark toward your success."

- Paul Matthews, Voice Talent

PREFACE

Strap in, because this is going to be a fun and informative ride.

This is about the incredibly awesome and respectable career choice called *voiceovers*, how you can start a career providing them, and ultimately, become tremendously successful at them.

Voiceovers have rocked my world and changed my life.

Who am I? I am Joshua Alexander (said in my best "I'm Batman" voice.) Without going too much in-depth here, I'll refer you to the "About the Author" section. Suffice it to say that I want this book to be about how you get properly started in voiceovers, as opposed to being about me.

However, briefly…

I am a middle-aged guy who's been doing voiceovers off and on since 1993, and full time since 2007. I finally made the jump to doing voiceovers as a service unto itself in 2016. Up until that point I had been (and still am) a successful multimedia businessman who ran five different companies from the comfort of his home. Now, it sometimes takes money to make money, and so my situation is a bit unique, as I had money going into voiceovers. Before I ever launched out into doing them full time (I was only offering them as an add-on to existing corporate videography for so many years until then), I had already generated over a million dollars in revenue from my multimedia production company. Therefore, my situation is not tremendously representative of the overwhelming majority of those seeking to enter into voiceovers. In many ways, I am an anomaly. Because of this, I promise to approach everything I describe from as much of a layman perspective as possible.

I've been very successful in multimedia and voiceovers, and that success is what motivates me to write. It is what *enables* me to do so. I blog prolifically, and my writings can be found in LinkedIn articles, on Medium.com, on Tumblr, on Facebook, and wherever else they're floating around the ether of the Interwebs. Voiceovers are my heart's desire (that and Bottle Caps candy – oh yeah, oops:

and my wife and kids too) and, as such, it was my heart's desire to write more about them. I love blogging and writing: it's my goal to be the Dave Barry of voiceover bloggers and authors, offering good quality satire and lightening the load through edutainment.

The author of this book has been a telemarketer, a Dairy Queen clerk, an office manager, an administrative assistant, an audio editor, a dispatcher, a Christian singer & speaker, a Jack in the Box worker, a paperboy, a corporate and wedding videographer, a service manager, a paperboy *again*, a voice talent, an artist, a poet, a business owner, a blogger, a graphic and web designer, and a dancer. I dropped dancing many years and many pounds ago when it became painfully obvious that I was about as graceful as a drunken lumbering Brachiosaurus traversing a field of marbles. I humbly acknowledge that God has given me some indisputable gifts. (Dancing is not one of them. Using mental telepathy on stoplights is.) I am deeply grateful and operate out of a profound sense of gratitude every day because of my gifts. You'll hear that as a constant and driven refrain throughout my book. I've had a lot of experience in a lot of areas since entering the workforce in 1988. I've worked at probably thirty different jobs. None of them will remember me, because I was the guy who wanted to be somewhere else. Who was *bound* to be somewhere else. Who actually *was* somewhere else sometimes, and that's why I was politely asked never to return.

So, back to this book…

Is this book about technique? No. It presumes you know at least *some* of the fundamentals of script-reading, but more importantly, are willing to *learn*, and be coached. That's why you purchased this book, or had it forced upon you by your wife who wants you to stop playing around and put some bread on the table.

It also presumes that you are probably non-union. Union-based voice talent are subject to a bit of a different life what with rules and structure and dues and everything that comes with being SAG-AFTRA. I'm non-union. However, the business lessons and tips in this book are pertinent to both sides of the aisle.

This is a book on taking that craft and putting it on a moving vehicle to take it somewhere: the vehicle of a successful business. More on coaching later, but here's what you'll learn from a great coach:

- Industry insights
- Mic placement & proximity
- Recommended hardware and software

- Technique
- Larynx care
- Target voiceover genre(s)
- Finding your "money voice"
- Demo production
- More

Please ensure that you don't skip coaching – it's so critical to your success in voiceovers!

Well, then, is this book about business development only? No. I certainly didn't want to be solely an informational writer: there are plenty of those out there already, and I'd just be joining the choir. Nay. I wanted to also bring some humor and some levity to your journey that is sometimes fraught with "rejection" (which is actually just selection) so that you can recharge at this pit-stop called laughter, and find strength to go another mile and send those auditions. So, know that you're embarking on an eclectic read that won't be just scholarly lecture-like. I deeply love Dave Barry, Steven Wright, Demetri Martin and Mitch Hedberg humor, and so some of my material – and definitely my blog at itsthevoicesinmyhead.com – is written in somewhat of a comical style to balance out the information overload that you may experience in other chapters. It's part biography, part anecdote, part instruction. But for the sake of simplicity, let us henceforth refer to it as "*bioanecstruction.*"

Conversely, it really, *really* impresses me when I develop a relationship with someone that is based on frequent exchanges of humor, when we finally sit down and have a cup of coffee together and there it is: that immense cavernous well of depth that they possessed, which I had to date received only hints of. People are *so* interesting, and there is so much more than meets the eye. I hate having one without the other. Purely shallow comedic exchanges leave you craving more connection and depth; too much emphasis on the heavy depth leaves you wanting to come up for air. So, this book offers both some comedic interludes *and* business insight to give you that well-rounded view.

I regard my situation humbly. When I'm following in the footsteps of people like J Michael Collins, Marc Cashman, Tom Dheere, Bill DeWees, Scott Burns, Pat Fraley, Tracy Lindley, Elaine Clark, and Paul Strikwerda, I don't know what I can truthfully add to the babble (because that's what we do all day) of voices that hasn't already been mentioned somewhere along the line. But I'm sure going to try. After all, I'm a try-er. Especially of patience. Ask my wife. I have never really played by the rules. I don't like rules. See? That's me driving over there on the other side of the highway with the crap-eating grin on my face. Wave! Wave to the nice men with the handcuffs driving right behind me! Such nice men with handcuffs.

I tend to buck the establishment and try the *Kobiyashi Maru*[1] approach. I'm unconventional that way, and thus, may seem controversial at times. I'm ok with it. My motto in business has always been "adapt and overcome."

Case in point: in 2007 I was besieged by a Craigslist flagger who decided to for whatever reason single out my media production ads and flag them repeatedly for removal. This was prior to Craigslist revamping their flagging policies. This continued from January through March of 2007. After three months of frustration, it prompted me to create a brand-new *alternative* website for the very same services I was providing… and thus I created

> *Business is a serious thing, and while you can get by on levity, you can't advance without sincerity.*

different ads…and thus the flagger didn't even know those ads were mine…and thus he left me alone…and thus I said "thus" a lot.

Adapt and overcome.

The sad truth is that his email address (we engaged in delightfully angry dialogue after he intentionally reached out to lecture me about my postings) was *flagger.cl@gmail.com.* Talk about a pathetic identity: it was his *calling* to ruin others. The same is true of people on Reddit who, once you've posted a positive offer to help those seeking to learn about voiceovers, downvote your answer. Why on earth you would downvote a post seeking to help people is beyond me. Some people in this world simply perplex me, whether they're serial flaggers or downvoters.

It is an unfortunate reality that sad, skeptical cynics are so pervasive on social media that they'll do anything to subvert a good cause out of their own suspicious worldview. I guess it takes a wide variety of people to populate a planet. Oh well! I'll be over here adapting and overcoming while they're over there hating people.

You now hold this book in your hands because you're either:

A) exploring voiceovers for the first time, or
B) exploring *improving* your voiceover career

Either way, I applaud you. To quote that great prophet Obi-Wan Kenobi, "You've just taken your first step into a larger world."

This book is a diary of lessons learned. It's a collection of business tips and tricks. It's a compendium of everything I've learned in business to make me successful as a voice talent, and everything I employ today to make -and keep- me successful. And I've indeed been successful! At the time of this writing:

- I've generated over $2 million dollars in overall business since 2003, and over half a million dollars in voiceover income since 2016 alone.
- In July of 2019, I made finally more money in voiceovers n a month than in all other media production pursuits combined! I made $15,387.07....and all with no overhead.
- In my highest revenue month ever, I brought in $39,535,87 in voiceover income.
- In one week alone I reeled in *thirty-four* different voiceover jobs, between direct jobs, repeat customers, P2P ("pay to play") jobs, and pickups. Thirty-four in a single week!
- In another week, I brought in $10,594.
- It's been a slow ramp-up, but for the first time ever, I finally surpassed six figures in a single year in voiceovers by mid-September 2019. In 2020, I doubled what I had made the previous year.

All of this gets me very, very excited. It's insane! Sometimes I wake up laughing. I'm very excited about my future forecast, and being able to eat lobster for dinner every night, on voiceover money. In fact, the only thing that remains is to record voiceovers *while* eating lobster, at which point I will surely die from ecstasy.

I am *passionate* about life, and I am *passionate* about voiceovers. In essence, they've nothing short of rescued me from being trapped in a career I loathed. I was performing wedding videography, which is the same as floating in a pot of boiling acid and being forced to listen to Michael Bolton on a punishing loop. Voiceovers have also saved me from the 9-to-5 doldrums and ratcheted up my confidence and drive to succeed. I live, sleep, eat, drink, and breathe voiceovers.

Nothing has ever motivated me like voiceovers have, and it's to the point where I loathe Friday afternoons (because the workweek is ending) and I am leg-shakingly excited on Sunday evenings (because the workweek is about to start). Wow. In fact, if you hover over me when I'm sleeping, and say the word "voiceovers", I'm sure to wake up with a jubilant thrill! Several people have been arrested for trying: it's been entertaining! Such nice men with handcuffs.

What I love about self-employment is that it's *mine*. No one can take it from me. I rise and fall on my own merits, and whether or not I succeed is completely up to me, not my employer's paycheck. I am pursuing *my* dreams, not my employer's. That, to me, is something I will never willingly trade, and you'd have to pry from my cold, dead, MKH416-gripping hands.

It's my hope that the book I'm writing is filled to the brim with new and exciting material, and of course great humor. But in truth, I can only draw upon those who have gone before me, and couple that with the very best of what I know. So, do me a favor and pretend to be excited if you hear something that's been heard before, and I'll promise to Thesaurus-it-up to give it a fresh spin for you, and try to perhaps make it a little more memorable. Business is a serious thing, and while you can get by on levity, you can't genuinely advance without intentionality.

It is with great deference and respect that I undertake to write about voiceovers and share it with you, because I'm treading on sacred ground of learning, and in that sacred process, *yea verily*, the student becometh the teacher.

Am I qualified to speak on voiceovers, and running a voiceover business? My numbers don't lie: the truth is yes. I've been asked to speak at great conferences, I've been interviewed countless times. I am constantly thanked by budding and established voiceover talent the world over. I'm asked to review demos and direct entrepreneurs in business. I've been the voice of many Fortune 500 companies on TV, on the radio, and on the web. I acknowledge all of that with a massive dose of humility and honor. I will go forth humbly and with honor, and with great cognizance that the ones who went before me equipped me to write the very book I'm writing, and I draw from them in the sharing.

The last thing I would say in terms of a bit of a disclaimer is that this book is written from my perspective. It is what has worked for *me*; it may not necessarily work for you. In fact, it's guaranteed to *not* work for many people, because no one is quite like me (can I hear an amen), and no one has the same makeup that I do.

I operate how I operate and have perfected my approach to code of conduct that works in tandem with my own makeup, which is a lovely shade of rouge, with thick mascara, enabling me to bat my eyes at you and make you, in the words of Antonio Banderas, ess-swoon.

Voiceovers is an industry that has drastically changed and been upended. Some say in a bad way, some say in a good way. And even more say in a *weird* way. With the advent of the Internet, home studios have sprung up in every corner of the planet, and everyone is a voiceover artist. It is a very, very easy industry to enter…and a very difficult industry to get right…unless you have direction and are highly committed to your dream.

My friend, the wonderful voiceover artist and author Paul Strikwerda, highlights the difference between those interested and those committed:

> *"The interested person is merely exploring options. The committed person is going for it. The interested person says: 'I'd like to,' 'I'm thinking of' 'It would be nice…" The committed person says 'This is my path,' 'This is my passion,' 'Nothing can stop me.' The interested person reactively responds to opportunities. The committed person proactively creates opportunities. The interested person is not invested in the outcome. The committed person does whatever it takes to achieve the outcome. The interested person is conditioned to 'trying.' The committed person is conditioned to 'doing.' The interested person always has reasons. The committed person has results."*[2]

Everyone wants to hop on board The Love Train.

Many years ago, if you were a voice talent, you'd get a call from your agent who would say to you "Can you get in here right now, I have the role of a lifetime!" So, you'd drop everything, throw on (off?) your jammies, drive to the studio, record the audition, return home…and then wait. Ultimately, if you get the job, then you'd have to throw off (on?) your jammies, drive back out to the studio, record your part(s), then come home. And if they needed any punch-ins? *Jammies + drive + rerecord.* And if they needed any pickups? *Jammies + drive + rerecord.* Round and round you go.

Now, you just walk into your control room or office, hit record, go record, stop recording, name the files, upload, invoice, done and mic drop. Don't forget your jammies.

A sea change has come to the voiceover industry, revolutionizing and equipping thousands to pursue their dream of voiceovers. What does that mean for you? It means the same thing I try to convey in every blog I write, every workshop I give, every video consult I perform, every webinar I teach at, every book I produce, and every communication I utter in the name of voiceovers. It's four words:

YOU. CAN. DO. THIS.

You are a vertebrate, not an invertebrate. *pause for effect* Wait what? Yes, you heard me. You have spine. You have backbone. You have fortitude comprising your very frame.. You're not a slippery fish or a spineless coward. You have decided to pursue something *rife* with rejection, *fraught* with fear, and *simmering* in struggle. The struggle in voiceovers is real, but you can do this. I believe in you.

This book is about my own experiences, my own life, my own passion, my own insights, and my own joy, as seen through a business and career in voiceovers. And I want to share it with you! *Tres bien, no?* Will everything herein apply to you? Certainly not. Will it be a fun trek though? Most definitely.

I've *so* enjoyed writing it, and my fingers hurt from so much typing, but it's a good hurt. I hope you enjoy it too, because I couldn't wait to share it with all of you…for a small fee of course. (My wife feels that our children need to eat.)

And now I'll say to you what Glenne Headley's character *The Jackal* said in *Dirty Rotten Scoundrels*:

"Ready? Then let's go get 'em."

Just make sure to "go get 'em" on the correct side of the highway… I found that out the hard way. Such nice men with handcuffs.

CONTENTS

CHAPTER 1:
AND THEY'RE OFF!

Before you jump right into it and scream to the world from the rooftops, *"I'M GOING TO BE THE GALAXY'S GREATEST VOICEOVER TALENT AND THAT'S THAT! HEAR ME ROAR, WORLD!!!"* have you sat down and asked yourself if you really do have what it takes?

If not, are you willing to train, to learn, and to study, to get it?

Jeff Goldblum's character in Jurassic Park had a line that I will never forget. It goes as follows: "Yeah, yeah, but your scientists were so preoccupied with whether or not that they *could*, that they didn't stop to think if they *should.*" So I want to ask you from the very beginning to ask yourself, *should* you do this? You might very well be able to, but *should* you? Will it become a passing fancy? Or might you spend so much money in it and ultimately be unsuccessful, angry, and in debt? All things to consider before launching out into this field.

With that said, let me congratulate you on even *considering* taking such an awesome plunge. You're about to dive into a pool full of wonder, great accomplishment, hopes fulfilled, character-driven flamboyancy, awesome networking, incredible dreams realized, and endless possibilities of being chosen.

There are plenty of genres you can pursue in voiceovers. You can pursue:

- Commercial work
- Explainer videos
- Narration, such as of documentaries
- E-Learning
- Character & Animation work
- ADR (Automated Dialogue Replacement)
- Audiobooks

- IVR (phone tree) recordings
- Overhead announcements for live events
- Podcast intros
- Political
- Other Web videos
- And many more!

Voiceovers is a behemoth of an industry, continually poised for growth despite the threats to it such as AI voices and the erosion of the industry pay scale. Regarding AI voices, even as Alexa, Siri and other assistive apps have grown in popularity, the truth is that people still prefer the emotional connection of a real human voice[3].

In 2017, there was a reported 900 percent increase in the number of "voiceovers required to be voiced" over the span of the previous three years. The e-learning market is expected to grow to be worth over $200 billion by 2024.[4]

"How do I get started in Voiceovers?" is a question that has been asked by thousands and thousands of people over the past few decades. Home studios crop up all the time and voiceover artists dot the planet numbering in the hundreds of thousands. And that question has been answered by many of these people with "I did it, and it worked."

Maybe you're asking this question because you've been told "you have a good voice." Many people have expressed to me that people have told them that. I want to start by saying something that might surprise you. Here it is: *"So what?"* And yes, I meant to say that. Is it a mean question? Not really, when you think about it. Every field needs to validate its entrants, and the voiceover industry is no exception.

Do you have an awesome voice? Maybe. Maybe you've been told you have a "face for radio" (yuk yuk yuk). *But an awesome voice does not a good voiceover artist make.* So, with that said, what *does* make a good voiceover artist? If you were going to bake a delicious batch of voiceover artist cookies, here are the ingredients you would pour in, in heavy doses:

- Resilience
- A lot of skill
- The ability to network
- A sense of humor
- The willingness to fail...and then try again
- Allowing yourself to be coached and trained

- Business acumen
- Mastering technique
- Listening
- Imparting
- Reading ahead
- Being passionate
- Lifting words off of the page
- Determination
- Grit
- Foresight
- Planning
- Marketing
- and most of all, being committed to goals.

GOALS & GROWTH

If you have a goal of growing a successful voiceover business, then you must check out my video training series, or my book series. They are minimal investments to ensure that you start off with the right inspiration and information. Both are available for purchase at www.supervoiceoverservices.com.

But here's what I say, and many would agree. The very first thing that you need to do is contact a voiceover coach. Don't wait. Check out Scott Burns today at www.bookscottburns.com. He'll give it to you straight, he'll tell you how it is, and he's incredibly generous with his time, his humor, and his passion. His rates are reasonable, and he's a wonderful mammal. You would do very well to learn from Scott. After all, he's my coach, and I speak from experience.

Remember this formula well:

Coaching > Demo > Website > Marketing

Get coaching. *Get instruction on how to do this right*. Everything else hinges on that. Do NOT skip coaching. Then have a demo made by that coach. Then have a website made when you've got a viable demo to present. Then, start telling people. Follow this foundation, and you'll succeed.

Scott will tell you if you have what it takes...and if you don't, he'll help you get there.

Aside from that, network with other voice talent. Join groups online. There are Facebook groups aplenty like VO Tech Talk[5], VO

Peeps[6], Global Voiceover Artists Network[7], and more. There are coaches, experienced voice talent and audiophiles like Scott Burns, Paul Strikwerda, Tim Tippets, Tracy Lindley, Marc Cashman, Everett Oliver, Pat Fraley, Dave Fennoy, J Michael Collins, Anne Ganguzza, Jon Bailey, Kay Bess, and many, many more, who would be willing to sow into your lives.

Join local voiceover Meetups. Talk with others in online communities. Network, network, network. Rub shoulders with greatness, and greatness will rub off on you.

DON'T QUIT YOUR DAY JOB

Ever heard that phrase? Lots of people the world over have been told "don't quit your day job." It's a phrase that is not meant to deter, and is often said in a spirit of humor. Ultimately, lots of actors (voice and regular actors alike) have to find a way to pay the bills. And voice acting won't do that right out of the gate. Ever heard the label "Starving Artist"? Mm-hmm.

> *Do NOT skip coaching. Then have a demo made by that coach. Then have a website made when you've got a viable demo to present. Then, start telling people. Follow this foundation, and you'll succeed.*

There are celebrities in the voiceover world who make a *fortune* and an absolute *killing* in voiceovers. There are legends, whose voice you've heard in movie trailers. Or master voice talent who may have held you captive, spellbound, as they have narrated an audiobook to you.

All of these people have invested into their craft, and spent countless time and dollars perfecting what they do and how they do it. Their names are fairly synonymous with celebrity, because they've paved the way.

But they didn't just make a killing in voiceovers right away. They worked very hard to pay for the things that they needed, such as equipment, coaching, software, training, and marketing. So, after a coach, remember that you need to make sure to find a way to pay for the things that you're going to need to be successful in voiceovers. To do that, you're going to need to make or save some cash, and invest that right back into your career.

I've heard it said that a career in cosmetology costs you between fifteen and twenty-five thousand dollars. And what do you get paid for a haircut? $18? $40? $60? You can voice a national television commercial in a directed session requiring about 30 minutes, provide them the raw audio and not need to do any pickups (changes) or even touching it up, for thousands and thousands of dollars.

Which one will you choose? Take your time; I'll be here when you come to your senses. A career in voiceovers is incredibly lucrative.

ARE YOU A SELF-PROMOTER?

There's nothing wrong with a little shameless self-promotion here and there. In this industry, the clients aren't going to necessarily find you. You have to work to find *them*. You have to *humbly put aside your humble*. Stick your chest out. Inhale deeply and know that you're a force to be reckoned with. After all, will the sheepish "Uh, sorry to bother you, but I was wondering if _____" approach get you anywhere? Methinks not.

Know deep inside, or at least start down the *path* of knowing and accepting, that you are a contender. That you are talented, and have something to offer. That you can contribute and help bring a company's message to life as their brand ambassador. There is nothing outside of the realm of possibility when you take on this mantle and don this cape. You are a *Voiceover Superhero*. Believe it right now.

Take the time to figure out where and how you're going to market, and know that there are people who will help you. I'm one of them. A paid way to go would be my video training series for voice talent that I mentioned earlier. It's, ahem, *really* good. It's not an expense; rather, it's an investment. Consider it...because it will change your marketing and business approaches.

Be bold. Know that you're in the ring and you have something to offer.

YOO-HOO! VOICEOVER WORK....
OLLIE OLLIE IN COME FREE!

So where is all this VO work that you've heard so much about? Where can you find it? Where is it hiding? The answer:

everywhere you look. You might be surprised to know that your company-owning uncle needs to have a new IVR (Interactive Voice Recording) system put in place for his business. Or that your dentist just had a promo video produced and needs narration. Or your sister's company is producing E-Learning and needs a voice.

Voiceover. Work. Is. Everywhere.

Look for it, because it's out there waiting for you to find. All you have to do is to look:

- The Voiceover Marketplaces - Voice123, Voices, VOPlanet, Bodalgo, Voiceovers, ACX, etc., as well as the newest marketplace as of March 2021, CastVoices. This is a HUGE topic I cover in an online blog[8] and a later chapter in this book, and needs to be handled with grace and thought, so do read that. This is the easiest way to get work if you're non-union. Keep away from sites like The Voice Realm, Fiverr, SpeedySpots, JustSaySpots, and GigNewton, etc. Bargain basement pricing coupled with some juvenile mistreatment of voice talent = a recipe for failure and frustration... and in some extreme cases, getting blacklisted.
- LinkedIn
- Instagram
- Facebook
- Google Ads
- Craigslist
- Vimeo
- YouTube
- Voiceacting.boards.net
- SearchTempest
- Stage32
- Reddit
- Tumblr
- Twitter
- Direct Emails
- Blog posts & outreaches
- Instagram ads
- Facebook ads
- Local networking groups such as Meetup, BizBuilders, LeTip, BNI, and Chambers of Commerce.
- Video Producer directories
- Casting agent directories
- Video production company websites
- Talk to other VO talent about where they get their work

- The phone book. (Huh???) Yes. The phone book. And you don't even have to be a telemarketer.

Everywhere you look, possible clients are swarming around you, under your nose, rubbing shoulders with you, sitting next to you, driving in front of you (or tailgating you), on the bus with you, on the phone with you, *in your life with you*. Voiceovers can be plugged into every area of your life. One of the best ways you can reach out is by getting vinyl lettering on your car...or having branded T-Shirts made that instruct people to "ask me about voiceovers." Seriously! Think I'm crazy? I've done both, and I've driven that car and worn that T-shirt out *on date night*. You never know who you might run into - and even if it's not a business prospect, what better subject to talk about than your exciting career?? (Or perhaps your amazing children, time permitting...)

Seriously, they're all out there. And my wife even lets me wear that shirt on date night without getting angry.

OOPS - I NEED EQUIPMENT TOO

Let's talk about equipment and software. Here's what I bought. This is *not* the end-all-be-all, nor is it exhaustive. This is simply what I bought for me, and how I roll. I've upgraded here and there, and purchased different equipment and software:

- Sony Vegas Pro 15 - I used to be a video editor, so this is what I started out with, as it has a great audio editing interface and allows for a plug-in chain on each channel
- I then upgraded to iZotope RX6 Advanced audio editing software
- I then upgraded to Reaper audio editing software for $60. SIXTY DOLLARS. An incredible purchase that has made my career. It is nothing short of incredible, and easy to use. I no longer use Sony. I will never leave Reaper.
- Grace m101 PreAmp
- Yamaha HS5 reference monitors
- Acoustic foam
- Acoustic noise blankets
- Scarlet FocusRite 2x2 audio interface to connect with my computer
- AudioTechnica AT2020 mic
- I then upgraded to a Neumann TLM 102 mic from the sale of my AT2020

- I then upgraded to a Sennheiser MKH416 mic from the sale of my Neumann.
- I then purchased a Neumann TLM 103 to use alongside my MKH416.
- Vocal Booth To Go for mobile recording
- Sennheiser HD 280 Pro Headphones
- Lyx Pro Headphones
- Started in an acoustically-treated closet.
- I then had a custom-built corner booth built in our former home for $1800
- I then upgraded to a StudioBricks home studio for $8000

As far as mic and equipment, you can get a great mic like a Rode NT1A, an AudioTechnica 2020 or 2035 (or even a 4040), an Apogee Mic 96k, Rode NT-USB, MXL 990s, Neumann TLM102 or TLM103, Shure SM7B, etc. However, I would caution you against using USB mics such as the Apogee: they're generally not as robust, and they bypass an important element such as your interface. Avoid cheapo mics. Kaotica Eyeballs. Blue Yeti models. Zingyoo. They're just not worth it, and producers can hear bad equipment.

Speaking of interface, I'd recommend a Scarlet Focusrite 2i2 interface, or an Audient ID4. Or a Presonus AudioBox. Of course, it goes without saying to get a great pair of reference monitors that allow you to really hear your material crystal clear. I love my Yamaha HS5's.

What I might recommend starting out is the following, for the budget-conscious:

- AudioTechnica 2020 - $169
- Mic & headphone cables - <$50
- Reaper - $60
- Scarlet FocusRite Solo interface - $109
- Decent headphones (LyxPro is a good inexpensive set of headphones) - $50
- Acoustically-treated space like a padded clothes closet - $50?
- Computer or laptop for editing - price varies

Check out BoothJunkie's YouTube channel[9] for information on building a great booth from scratch!

Want to have someone check out your audio and make sure it's up to snuff? Check with Jordan Reynolds[10], George Whittam and Dan Lenard[11], Tim Tippets[12], or Uncle Roy Yokelson[13].

Now. That little thing called "Business Savvy". This is where a lot of voice talent fall short and drop off the map. Business savvy. Acumen. Do you know what it means?

What does it take for you to run a successful business? Surely, you can't run it with just your voice. You need a system in place *around* your voice to ensure that that beautiful little product you're trying so hard to peddle is getting heard, getting estimated properly, getting invoiced properly, and reaching people. You need to have a structure around this enterprise called "my voice."

Over the years, I had a Microsoft Access database designed, and I've improved upon it over and over throughout the years. It runs my business. All of my information is in there. I can see how many people I've estimated and how many people I've actually booked. I can see my marketing ROI. I can see my income. I can see how much I've got to pay in taxes. I know which of my ad sources are bringing in the most money. I know which voiceover marketplace, which customer, which agent is bringing me the most money.

I've invested back into it over and over again - and that's a key point, all of this is an *investment*, not an expense - and now it's everything. It's part-CRM, part-accounting, part-marketing. It's truly amazing. I also designed stationery. This includes:

- Business cards
- Logo
- Invoice templates
- Estimate templates
- Glossies
- T-Shirts
- Bumper Stickers
- Thank you cards
- Flyers

I've needed to treat my business *like a business*. If I treat it like a hobby, it's destined to fail. If I treat it like a business, I can make some very good revenue. There's a huge chasm of difference between some extra chump change, and genuine hard-earned, measurable revenue. One is a side hustle; the other is a thriving enterprise.

You need to think about what your *business* is going to look like. Can you envision yourself as, instead of a voice talent, a successful businessperson who just *happens* to do voiceovers? If you can do the latter, you're going places. Remember: *failing to plan is planning to fail.*

DO I NEED TO BE UNION OR NON-UNION?

Now, let's not put the cart before the horse. You don't want to even approach agents or producers yet. Get yourself some coaching, then demos, then a website, and then establish yourself, and *then* market yourself to agents and producers. Remember the formula I mentioned before.

The short answer is that when you're ready, you don't "need" to join a union. There's no requirement. If you're union, you open yourself up to having to pay dues...*but*...you also open yourself up to some potentially super high-paying jobs...and some good health benefits. But if you're non-union, you just may chance upon some of those super-high paying jobs as well (I have), there are no dues, and there is much more work available to you. Much.

There are some exclusivity problems with doing both, so navigate this field carefully. You are under no obligation to join a union. In fact, the overwhelming amount of voice talent out there are non-union, and are making a great annual income soliciting and finding their own work.

Again, there is no requirement to being union, and you're not limited. The main drawback is that if you're union, and you're starting out, remember - there are talent in that union pool who have been talent *forever* - and a lot of these agencies know them, love them, and are used to them. You'll be trying to carve out some space for yourself in what is commonly referred to as granite. So, good luck there.

WHAT'S YOUR NEXT MOVE?

Get some great books to help you learn! These are some *super* books available out there:

- *Making Money in Your PJs* by Paul Strikwerda[14]
- *Voice-Over Voice Actor* by Yuri Lowenthal and Tara Platt[15]
- *V-Oh!* by Marc Cashman[16]
- *The Art of Voice Acting* by James R Alburger[17]
- *How to start and build a 6-Figure Voiceover Business* by Bill DeWees[18]

- *The Voiceover Startup Guide* by Chris Agos[19]
- *Voice Over Man* by Peter Dickson[20]
- *Voiceover Achiever* by Celia Siegel[21]
- *The Super Voiceover Artist Series* by Yours Truly[22]

And remember what I said? Contact Scott Burns, or another vetted coach, and get quality coaching. That's your very first step. Scott is a fantastic coach. And there are others just like him who want to invest into your life. When I first launched solely into voiceovers (after having done them as part of other projects for close to three decades) I was so shocked to find such a community of such sustained support, and an environment of help out there.

Voice talent genuinely want other voice talent to succeed! It's such a strange industry that way - where you encourage your competitor to get a job that you're in the running for. Plumbers don't do that. Automotive shops don't do that. Electricians don't do that. Realtors don't do that.

Just know that you can do this. The caveat is that you both have an equal footing. Just because Joe Voiceover has 26 years' experience, and you have 26 minutes', doesn't automatically grant Joe Voiceover *fait accompli*. The client just may have *your* voice in their heads...not Mr. Voiceover's, regardless of your lack of experience. If you sound like you can lift those words right off the page and breathe life into them, and not sound like you're reading, then you just might beat out an industry pro.

This is an industry that is tremendous fun. There are incredible annual events and conferences like *VO Atlanta* and *WOVO-Con*. You can join regular local voiceover Meetups and be inspired by your fellow colleagues and this mutual race of shared joy and pursuit. Cheer on and be cheered! Encourage and be encouraged! Voiceovers are a rewarding career on a number of levels, even before you score your first job.

Why?

The benefits of being a voiceover artist:

- Work from home
- Work as much or as little as you like
- Set your own hours
- Spend time with your family and your own pursuits
- Have a career that you can call your own
- Be creative
- Call your own shots

- Choose your own clients
- Constantly grow and innovate in performing and marketing
- Take longer-than-two-week vacations
- And, the most awesomest....work in your underwear. (Ew.)

Sound appealing? It should. It's the best life ever.

You can check out my full list of services and products I offer on my "Services"[23] page, all available to help you in your growth of running a voiceover business.

I hope this answers the question "How do I get started in voiceovers?" for you. Ultimately, just start. It's fun in this sandbox.

All this goes without saying that this is from *my* experience. Everyone's experiences are unique to *them.* However, if you would like a much more robust experience than this one - and a much longer, comprehensive resource guide - check out Dee Bradley Baker's "All to Know about Going Pro in VO".[24]

AUDITIONING

Now let's talk about auditioning a bit. When we audition, do we count on actually being cast in that role? Is it something that we really want? Or are we just rapid firing out multiple auditions so that we'll *maybe* get something here and there, hedging our bets as it were, so that it will *kind of* work out for us one way or another? Casting a super wide net to reel in at least one minnow? Paul Strikwerda offers the following: "If your custom demo (audition) sounds too rushed, you won't be considered. If you take too much time to perfect every second, you'll miss the boat."[25] It's about balance.

I recently had a conversation with a colleague, and they were telling me that they don't ever really give their "all" during an audition; they save it for the actual read. I had to scoff at their logic, for obvious reasons. I literally made a scoff sound, which sounds something like a cross between a gag and a profound urge to pee.

Huh? Saving it for the actual read? *Mon ami,* you'll never get to the actual read without giving it your *all* to get there.

You can't get a 100% job from a 50% audition.

THE PRODUCER'S CHAIR

Let's look at it from the producer's perspective for a moment. You know they're developing audition fatigue as they go through the onslaught of submitted auditions. You know they're losing the will to live as they *next-next-next* their way through scores of them. Is it reasonable to assume that you, appearing in their lineup with your half-baked and noncommittal audition, are going to make the slightest impression on their casting choice?

They say there's a "lead line." Michael Bell says the following:

One thing I've learned is that your VO audition must capture the casting director's attention in the first 10 seconds or they will not listen to the rest. They simply don't have time.[26]

And he's right. If you don't, you're a goner. You're literally *dead in the water*, and the producer will never even remember your name. You'll never even get to the "Money Line" (as Bill DeWees calls it)[27] before you're shot down.

But how about this. How about if you, with all of your muster and luster and bluster, can take that audition, supercharge it, and make such an impression that they have no choice but to remember you?

Your goal is to knock 'em dead. Not to knock 'em somewhat sleepy.

ALL OR NUTTIN'

Armageddon. Lord of the Rings. Mission Impossible. Raiders of the Lost Ark. The Empire Strikes Back. Cujo. Close Encounters of the Third Kind. Taken. Tootsie. Aliens. Meet the Parents. E.T.. Finding Nemo. Star Wars. Blair Witch Project. It's a Wonderful Life. The Goonies.

Name *any* movie, and you will recognize that there's a plot. A goal. An important mission. The protagonist(s) in any movie has a task that they must accomplish, and they must go on a journey of self-discovery in order to get there. They have to go on a journey of change; they have to grow and learn. They're committed to their goal and their mission.

> *Your goal is to knock 'em dead. Not to knock 'em somewhat sleepy.*

Just because you're not in the movie yet, should your audition be with any less feeling?

Remember *The Return of the* King, the movie? I will never forget on the last scenes. Sam and Frodo are halfway up Mount Doom. Sam says to a fading Frodo, "C'mon, Mr. Frodo. I can't carry it for you. But I can carry you! *Come on!*" And Sam slings Frodo over his shoulder and carries him all the way up Mount Doom. Half-baked food doesn't taste very good. Half-assed attempts don't resonate with anyone.

If your goal is to get in, why would you be content with just quietly knocking at the front door?

There's so much more to say on this – but is there? Is it really necessary? It's simple. There's no getting around it. You can't *almost* your way into a role. You can't *kind of* do it. You *intend* your way into a role. Otherwise, you intend your way into frustration.

I HAVE A LOT TO GIVE.
SO, HERE'S A TINY LITTLE BIT

Every role, every time, in every way, requires everything you've got. You've paid that membership to that P2P (pay-to-play voiceover marketplace). You've contacted that client and swore that you could do something marvelous. So, live up to your investment and promise.

Chew on these examples:

- Baseball's heavy hitters don't swing for the infield, hoping to lazy-lob one.
- Wide receivers don't race across the field, planning to run underneath the ball without raising their arms to catch it.
- Basketball players don't charge down the court, wanting to just stand under the hoop.
- Politicians don't run for the presidency just so they can increase their Twitter followers.
- Top chefs don't strive to make the best Top Ramen.
- Tourists don't go to Rome and hope to avoid the Coliseum.
- Fishermen don't cast their line out, wishing for minnows.
- The Beatles didn't take their music to America, desiring to play only in garages and talent shows.

Voiceover artists don't hope to do a mildly acceptable job. Is it risky to give your all and put yourself out there? Sure. But the cold truth? You have more to risk by *not* risking.

It's called giving your *all*. It's called going the distance. They call it 100%. There's no such thing as conserving your energy in auditions. The audition maketh the job. Go forth therefore, and give thou in all thy fullness! *disengages King James mode*

STREAMLINE YOUR PROCESS

Streamline your auditions! Don't spend precious minutes, hours, whatever, endlessly recording and re-recording and then editing and re-editing. Get a program like Reaper, where you can have automation. (And if you would like a complete training course on streamlining your workflow in Reaper, visit my training course at supervoiceovertraining.com.) Get a program like Pro Tools, Adobe Audition, TwistedWave, Logic Pro X, or any DAW (Digital Audio Workstation) with multiple channels that you can program a plug-in stack on, and that is ready to go. All of your audio is instantly manipulated to being broadcast-ready *while* you review it, in real-time. That way, you're not tweaking and *re*-tweaking and spinning your wheels doing all of that stuff. You want to get into your booth to record your auditions, get out, edit them and send right away, rinse and repeat.

The faster you can crank out those auditions (while doing a great job on them of course), the higher up you are going to be in a potential client's listening lineup, and thus the higher up your odds go of being officially cast in a role. Before these producers develop what could be called "audition fatigue", you want to get your audition into their hot little ears, before they are tired of listening to all these people and are now screaming "just pick one!"

Don't get stuck in analysis paralysis. Don't spin your wheels on your audition or editing process. Trust yourself, do well, develop a template and stick to it. Streamline your workflow, streamline your audition process, get them done, and get them out.

CHAPTER 2:
VOICEOVERS:
A HORRIBLE HOBBY

THE HOBBY OF VOICEOVERS

When you think of a hobby, what comes to mind?

- Playing the drums?
- Sculpting clay?
- Writing poetry?
- Calligraphy?
- Painting?
- Building suspension bridges in your backyard?[28]
- Collecting baseball cards?

What is a hobby, after all, but a pastime? Just that. Something to pass the time. It holds no significant value other than personal fulfillment – which I'm not knocking by the way; we need that! – but a hobby brings nothing to your budget; rather it brings *expense* for materials, or training, or other supplies needed to enjoy said hobby. Nothing is added to your career forecast other than a carved-out piece of your schedule dedicated to enjoyment.

> *Expenses take care of a short-term need; investments produce returns and dividends.*

Voiceovers, as a hobby, can bring a lot of fulfillment.

They can also *deprive* you of fulfillment. You can settle on the nickel and miss the dollar. They can bring you some measure of satisfaction, and rob you of utter contentment. They can pass the time, and in the same stretch, steal your time, never to return it in the long run.

So, enjoy your voiceover hobby! I pray you have fun with it! I hope that it's fulfilling for three weeks, or six months, or perhaps two years. I expect that you'll thoroughly enjoy it and that it fulfills you.

And I pray that you drop it as a hobby like a hot potato.

THE BUSINESS OF VOICEOVERS

If you choose to pursue voiceovers as a hobby, God bless you. No one could blame you: after all, it certainly is an enjoyable one! Hey, you might even make $20 from a project! *(Which, by the way, is what some of the clients on Fiverr are counting on you to say...)*

Or...you could make $5000. Plus residuals. Plus name recognition. Plus connections to future clients and other voiceover jobs in abundance. Plus plus plus.

A hobby brings you temporary fulfillment; a business brings you increasing provision.

Hobbies and crafts are essential for our contentment. Forest Hill Retirement says that they lower the heart rate.[29] They bring us balance and health. They give us the ability to unplug. For me, I sing, I blog, I swim, I run, and I build Lego spaceships with my son. OK, the honest truth is that he's asleep and I've commandeered them to add another sick Lego spaceship to my sick fleet.

But...

What if you could unplug from your 9 to 5, and you could instead make a living off of your "hobby?" What if you could convert it into a business?

- What if instead of buying craft materials, you could buy a business license?
- What if instead of purchasing a Blue Yeti microphone, you could purchase a Sennheiser MKH416 or a Neumann TLM103? Or an AKG C-214 or 414? Or a Rode NT1A? Or what if someday you were able to buy a Neumann U87?
- What if instead of recording in your closet, you could record in StudioBricks, WhisperRoom or VocalBooth?

If you truly treat expenses (short term) as investments (long term), you'll go far. Everything that you expend with voiceovers, divesting yourself of finances *today* for something that is an investment into your *tomorrow*, is a decision that catapults you forward into the far future of your progress. You're saying, essentially, "I believe in myself and my abilities to produce this money back, and to in fact grow a money tree that will continue to bear fruit for myself, because of this one [insert purchase here]." Some of your investments are veritable time machines, taking you from here to there in the timeline of quality, leapfrogging intermediate purchases you might have made.

Expenses take care of a short-term need; investments produce returns and dividends.

Again, you might make $5 on Fiverr (aka the F-Word in the Voiceover industry) or $20 on Justsayspots or $100 on The Voice Realm. These base sites are horrible and corrosive to the voiceover industry. On that note, if you're wanting to succeed in the voiceover industry, you'll avoid these three sites in particular like the Bubonic plague. But with voiceovers as a business, you could gain direct clients for yourself through marketing, and secure a client that will bring you multiple thousands of dollars worth of work per year… half-year…quarter… or even month!

Let me tell you what I see when someone on Fiverr states that they will do your 1000-word voiceover for $20. I see *desperation*. I see inexperience. I see lack of knowledge of the industry pay scale. I see sheepishness. I see lack of self-respect. I see "not a team player." But there's no way to police such activity, and it's truly a free country.

However – the main point I'm making here is just to not worry about such offerings. It's not my job or interest to police these people. In this vast universe of the internet, with so many players playing the game, all I can focus on is me, and I want to offer quality offerings at quality pricing, not quality offerings at bargain basement pricing. As Elaine Clark says, "If a talent gives away their services or undermines industry standard rates, they are sending a message that their services have little or no value. It may bring in jobs initially, but those buyers, once they have a budget, will go elsewhere for a higher-level performer."[30]

I recently had a disagreement with a lowballer in a voiceover group on Facebook who insisted that the price offering should be what the client can afford. Short of crying out "B___ S___!" I reminded them that *the price is the price is the price*, and referred them back to the GVAA Rate Guide. What you pay me for voiceovers

I never went into voiceovers with hope…I went in with intention.

does not depend on how much you make nor what your balance sheet is. It doesn't matter if you're nonprofit or a good cause. It doesn't matter how long I've been doing them, either. A voiceover service has a universal rate to everyone (based mostly on usage), and I choose to charge that universal rate.

What will your choice be? Everyone pays the same for an oil change, a plane flight, or a haircut. It's a service-based industry. There are corresponding market rates for such services. They're paying for the *service*, not your tenure in the service. Remember that. The service costs what the service costs. Period.

TREAT IT LIKE A BUSINESS

Again, I'm a businessman who *happens* to do voiceovers. I *love* voiceovers: they are my business, and they are my passion, because they not only bring me joy and fulfillment, they bring me great amounts of resource to provide for my family.

Let me list for you a few things that distinguish me as a voiceover businessman, as opposed to a voiceover hobbyist:

- I've created three voiceover websites to support my business
- I've invested thousands of dollars into a Studiobricks studio (and a custom-built studio prior to that one), Sennheiser microphone, Sennheiser and Neumann microphone, iZotope software, branded clothing, advertising expenses, and more
- I've attended local Meetups and Chambers of Commerce meetings to promote my business
- I obtained business licensing for myself
- I've labeled my car with vinyl lettering to attract business to myself
- I paid for a custom phone number
- I pay taxes on my voiceovers
- I am constantly seeking to expand my horizons
- Every day, I establish new relationships with potential clients
- I do this 9 to 5 every weekday, and beyond
- I wake up every day excited to go to work
- I've submitted nearly 30,000 auditions
- When I'm out and about, I make voice memos the instant a new idea comes to me for a blog…a live Instagram

video…a workshop…a follow-up note for a client…or a broadcast.
- I keep my finger on the pulse of my business by watching my VoiceZam player statistics[31] to see who is listening to my demo reels.
- Every single expense I make into voiceovers is not that. It is *not* an expense. It is an *investment*.
- I set and hit or exceed goals every week
- I invest time into blogging
- I help colleagues and provide free 20-minute voiceover video consults
- I invest a massive amount of time into marketing
- I've written several books on voiceovers
- I teach for free at voiceover conferences and webinars

I am a voiceover businessman because I choose to make this my business, not my hobby. Again, I never went into voiceovers with hope…I went in with *intention*. My first step was getting a business license. After that, I could successfully say "It's official!" It was never a hobby, but now it never would be. Yes, I thoroughly enjoy it as one would enjoy a hobby, but I will not relegate voiceovers to the category of hobby, because there is a huge well there that I can tap in order to bring massive provision to my family.

To relegate voiceovers to hobby status would be to ricochet off of, to momentarily touch and then leave, and no more, the wonder of a truly satisfying and lucrative career.

BEATING A DEAD HORSE

I'm just another voice (get it?) in this great choir when I share on this. There are many voiceover businessmen just like myself who just happen to do voiceovers, but they are first and foremost entrepreneurs. They understand that in order to succeed, you need structure, planning, goal-setting, etc.

You need drive, determination, and resilience. You need focus, clarity of vision, and aptitude. You must find what works best for you as a business, and then run with it. I don't mean to beat a dead horse, so I'll just chime in and say "What they said."

[pause for effect]

OK, I'll say even more.

Treat voiceovers like a business, make it official, and see yourself reap invaluable rewards heaped upon invaluable rewards.

I'll never forget the first time I was paid for a voiceover job. I thought to myself, "Holy smokes, it actually works!" I expected it to, but that feeling opened up Pandora's box within me. Simultaneously, I thought "It's possible." "This is it." "This is where my income will come from."

This system *does* work. It's not Amway, it's not a Ponzi scheme, and it's not a Kool-Aid stand. This is an official business that brings in billions of dollars a year in advertising and other forms of revenue for corporate videos, E-Learning, animation, Explainer videos, audiobooks, and more. You can share in those dollars! This system can pay your bills, your car payment, your mortgage, and then some. I'm living proof.

At the time of this writing, I am closing in on $600,000 in voiceovers in a little over 4 years of providing voiceovers full time. That's an average of $150,000 in exclusively voiceover income each year. And some months it is enough to pay our mortgage several times over. In fact, as of this writing, I've already been able to set aside funds allocated to our mortgage for the next eight months.

It *is* possible.

Go forth and conquer...with a business license.

CHAPTER 3: CREATING & SUSTAINING A THRIVING VO BUSINESS

MY STORY

We're going to dive into a lot of informative bits here that hopefully will give you lots of tips and tricks to run a successful voiceover business long-term.

I'm very humbled to be able to do what I do. I am extraordinarily grateful. It is a tremendous privilege to be able to perform, teach about and blog about voiceovers. They say, "find what you love to do, and you'll never work a day in your life." That's very, very true.

My day does not feel like work. It does not consist of work. Yes, there are activities that I do every day for the maintenance of my voiceover business. But none of it has ever felt like, "Oh, this is labor". My *wife* has gone through labor. *She* knows what labor is. *This ain't labor.* I absolutely love what I do. And it's a passion of mine. And so it's my privilege and my joy to share it with you.

Many of my esteemed voiceover colleagues know that I come from a career in wedding videography. I have essentially been rescued, delivered, so to speak, from a business that negatively impacted my life and sanity. *Hallelujah* for deliverance from bridezillas, groomzillas, momzillas, and all kinds of other -zillas.

Sure, wedding videography fit the bill for a while. It put food on our table. Ultimately it was productive and sustaining, but never emotionally satisfying in the way that voiceovers have been. So, I'm actually not doing that anymore, having given it up in 2018. And I am *so* grateful that I've no longer needed it.

How I got into voiceovers was kind of an accident. I was working at a telemarketing company in the early 90s, and I was selling PSAs (public service announcements) to local businesses that were sponsored on the radio: "good sound advice brought to you as a courtesy by Bob's plumbing." For example, "Talk to your kids about the dangers of drinking and driving." "Use a kid code to avoid abduction," etc. Good messages brought to them by local business leaders and business owners. I was just a salesperson. One client said, "I'll buy - but only if you read it on the air." They apparently liked me so much they wanted *me* to read it.

And so I said to my boss, "Wow, okay, well, he'll buy, but he wants *me* to read it! Can I read it? Hello???" My managers agreed, and I stepped into a studio for the first time. I said to myself, "I like this a *lot*." And it planted a seed in me for doing voiceovers, way back when.

> *If you think you can't do voiceovers as a career, if you think you're limited to doing it as a hobby, think again. There's a richness and a trove of business opportunities here that are just waiting for you. They're ripe for the picking.*

.   .   .

There's a richness and a trove of business opportunities here that are just waiting for you. They're ripe for the picking. It is possible with hard work and a little elbow grease, and with grit and gumption, tenacity and resolution.

I average between 200 and 250 auditions per week. That's right, I'll say that again. 200 to 250 auditions per week, as well as 150 marketing contacts per day. I treat auditions as marketing opportunities! Here's why:

1) It's very possible to get a job - that's the optimum end result.

2) The second result is you can not get that specific job, per se, but they can say "you actually would be perfect for our next script coming up". So, there's a second opportunity.

3) Thirdly, they can add you to their roster.

4) Or they can say, "you're not perfect for this one, but 'Bob's Explainer Videos' down the road - he does a lot of these - you'd be excellent for him." So, you get a job by referral, as it simply puts you in front of people who might add you to their roster as voiceover talent.

5) Fifthly, you get to refine your craft by working hard, perfecting auditions, and perfecting how to get under those words and lift them off the page and breathe *life* into them, taking each script and turning it into more practice.

So, as you can see, there are five possible beneficial outcomes for me that come from auditions. That's why I do so many per week. I want to get cast for these jobs. That's the ultimate goal.

I count *all* of these auditions as marketing opportunities, and I average between 10 and 20 jobs per week. One week I had 34 jobs!

I run the Global Voiceover Artist Network on Facebook; you can join us at www.gvoa.net. It's a thriving community with strong growth and great interaction between members. You can go there and ask questions on hardware, software, conferences, coaching, plugins, books, resources, technique, throat remedies, whatever. It's a great hive-mind of people prepared to contribute to your success, answer questions honestly, give you feedback on your demos, refer you to an excellent coach, etc. The GVAN is something I'm very proud of. It's a strong, thriving, growing community that is doing very well. Join us! We'd love to have you.

I've never once – to my recollection – been told, "hey, Josh, you've got a great voice. You should do voiceovers." I don't recall ever once having been told that. What I'd like for you to focus on in the first chapter of this series is being a *businessperson* first.

Again, I am a businessman who just *happens* to do voiceovers. In structure, ecosystem, branding, marketing, etc., you can be a contender in the VO marketplace, by treating it like a business.

I don't like to do a lot of audiobooks, but I have a client named Thibaut Meurisse. He is French. He's a wonderful author, in the vein of Anthony Robbins: personal motivation, speaker and author...he once said "*success is not an event, success is a process*".

What a fantastic quote! Success is a *journey*. This is a time-honored adage: "It's a marathon, not a sprint." It doesn't happen overnight like that. Success is a process by which you gradually become better, a process by which you evolve, by which you become someone who is knowledgeable and wise, pursuing everything the right way.

Success is not an event. Success is a process every time. You don't just all of the sudden have success. It is a process towards success, and to working towards goals to making yourself as successful as you possibly can. That is all a process; not an event.

SO HOW DO I TURN IT FROM A HOBBY TO A BUSINESS?

There seems to be this illusion that people refer to as "my big break." I'd like to dispel that myth and burst that bubble right from the start. Landing jobs, training others, giving critiques, being heard, and having your opinions valued – that's success. And that doesn't happen overnight. It is a *process*.

So, get the "big break" mentality out of your mind from the very beginning. Focus on building and on construction in this first phase, because you don't just *break into* voiceovers; you build and you get there, eventually. The business comes first, then your craft. You form a solid foundation for whatever craft you decide to pursue, or whatever vocation you choose to pursue, not the other way around.

You have to have a foundation in order for the craft to grow and to thrive. Looking at it another way, you have to have a vehicle to take your craft somewhere. That foundation and that vehicle is the structure of a business. Build your foundation first, and then build on that foundation.

There are five questions that you should ask yourself if you want to be successful in any entrepreneurial pursuit. Here they are:

1. Who are you? What makes you *you*?

2. What uniqueness do you bring to the table? Why should someone choose you over someone else? What attracts a client to you as opposed to another voice talent?

3. What makes you not just unique, but *better*? What makes you better for this job than all the *hordes* of other voice talent that are out there? What do you represent where they would say, "Well, there's all these guys, but then there's Joshua Alexander…he's our choice for this script"?

4. What did you *used* to do? Or what do you do now that you never want to do again? For me, that was wedding videography. Is there something that you do as a vocation, as a breadwinner? Something that provides for you that you just don't want to do anymore? This is an entrepreneurial

question. If you're trapped in a non-entrepreneurial pursuit, working for someone else's dream, you have to identify that and systematically plan to step away from it and make that crossover into voiceovers.

5.   Speaking of leap, are you prepared to *sacrifice* for your dream? One thing I'll talk about in this chapter and in other chapters is that you have to develop a mentality of expenses as *investments*. There are things that I bought that I did not consider as an "Okay, if I must" type of purchase.   They were critical.   My thoughts were, "I *must* have this for my future success. It is *critical* that I have this". Are you prepared to sacrifice for your dream?

If you have not had coaching in voiceovers, you need to stop what you're doing. Put this book down, or take it back to the clerk and ask for a refund. (Kidding. Don't do that please.) Go back to the drawing board and get coaching.

Now, I'm not a coach, and I'm not going to sell you on a coaching package and ask you to enter your credit card number here. That's not who I am. But it is highly recommended that you get coaching to know how to find your target genre. (You *can* pursue multiple genres as well.) You need a coach to help you learn how to read and sound like you're not reading, and learn how to get under those words and lift them all off the page, bringing them to life.

Coaching will help refine your already God-given reading ability into something that's compelling, something that is mysterious, deep, powerful, full and rich, and *believable*. A coach helps you do that. A coach can produce a demo, and you'll want those demos done professionally. Don't ever produce your own demos unless you are a seasoned audio production engineer who is receiving feedback from other seasoned audio production engineers. You don't produce your own demos because you're not impartial. You're not unbiased. You're going to sock yourself in the shoulder and say "*man*, that was good. What a great demo!" A producer, however, may receive it and say, "*Man*, that was awful! What a horrible demo!" You have someone *else* produce it, who is *impartial*, and can pull the best out of you that way. There's no getting around it: professional demo producers produce professional demos.

You start with coaching, you move on to demos, and then you move on to marketing and auditioning. Once you've got those tools in your toolkit – coaching and demos – *then* you start reaching out and sharing with the world what you can do.

I'm going to highly recommend a book that is not part of the VO "booksphere". It is called 'The E-Myth" by Michael Gerber. And it talks about three different roles that are indispensable for you in running a VO business, or any business. But as a VO business, it is essential that you employ all three of these roles. Now, you can outsource some of these things, sure. But you can never outsource the technician side of it. *You* are the one who is performing the work.

The three roles are technician, manager, entrepreneur.

The technician is the person who does the work. The manager is the one who runs the business. The entrepreneur is the one who has the vision for the future, and who lays the groundwork for growth, for prosperity, for a business plan of attack, for a mission statement, and for a mantra.

The E-Myth is such an excellent book! It is *loaded* with all kinds of insight as to why each role is critical. Again, yes, you can outsource, say, your marketing, to someone else. But unless you have a stake in *how* that marketing is done, then it's really not yours anymore. It belongs to someone else. You'd be outsourcing a very important component that allows you *personally* to connect with people, not someone else saying "Joshua Alexander is great". It's *you* saying, "Hi, I do voiceovers and I love them. And I'd love to work with you."

Get that book – I highly recommend it. Learn those three roles that will help you in your business.

A MANTRA FOR ANY ENTREPRENEUR

A business mantra is so essential for understanding who you are, what you offer, why you do what you do, and where you want to go. My mantra is something that unfortunately comes from one of the Star Wars movies that I like to pretend does not exist: *The Phantom Menace*. I just wish it would go away. It is *so* not part of my Star Wars canon. Be that as it may, the mantra is uttered by Qui Gon Jinn to a young Anakin Skywalker. He says the following:

Your focus determines your reality.

My friend, that is a powerful phrase, in any pursuit!

Remember Michael Phelps, professional Olympian swimmer? That man is made of steel! How many hours did he log in the pool prior to the Olympics? How many records and medals did he take home?

His focus determined his reality. All the pioneers in history: their focus determined their reality.

Make voiceovers your *focus*; become intent beyond any measure to make this a success. Tell yourself: I'm going to focus, I'm going to learn, I'm going to grow, I'm going to market, I'm going to brand, I'm going to practice, I'm going to get coaching, I'm going to take group coaching and teaching and refine my skills. I'm going to learn about how to run a business professionally. *Your focus determines your reality.* Never forget that.

> **Good is always the worst enemy of best.**

A mission statement is an excellent thing to have as well: to define your business and your pursuits that way, their reasons for doing what you do and how you do it. Very important from the start to have that. What things do you need to start your business and to actually treat it like a business? Where do you want to go? What do you want to be known for?

Here's my mission statement:

Joshua Alexander Voiceovers is dedicated to the utmost quality of voiceover delivery and performance in tandem with encouragement, affirmation, and exhortation that inspires, entertains, and motivates.

ALL KINDS OF BUSINESS TIPS

I've got a long list of random business tips that I'm going to run through. These are things that have been formative for me, and instrumental in my own success over the years. But the number one thing beyond anything else, and the foundation for being successful in anything? *Gratitude*. An attitude of gratitude.

If you were a fly on the wall in my office, every time I'm awarded a job, you will hear me say, "Thank You, Lord." I will say that every single time. Every time some client writes back and says, "Thank you for sending your demo", or "Yes, we'd love to put you on our roster": "Thank you." An attitude of gratitude. Whomever you want to thank is entirely up to you. But that attitude of gratitude lays the foundation for future success.

What comes around goes around! Call it *The Secret*: that phenomenon you saw on Oprah many years ago, whatever it is, whatever you're putting out there into the universe, back to God, however you're doing it: gratitude goes an incredibly long way towards having you reap a positive emotional and financial bounty in running your business.

Another thing that is indispensible is *intention*, not hope; intention trounces hope every time. There's a little printout on the outside of my studio door that says, "I've already been awarded all of these jobs." It's just a little phrase I have on my door that I see which puts me in a mindset of coming in, to conquer, to do well, to give it my all every time I'm going to do these auditions, that doesn't just pertain to auditions. It pertains to everything I do in business. I *intend* to succeed, I *intend* to buy this. I *intend* to accomplish these goals. Intention trounces hope! Don't tell yourself "I *hope* maybe I'll be a success one day, God permitting." That's wishful thinking, and there's nothing wrong with that in and of itself, but you need to have *intention* to see it take root and be grounded in that. Think "I *will* get this job."

Get a logo made! A logo gives you vision for who you are, and is part of your branding. A logo shows people what you stand for. I want people to see my little VO superhero logo, the same way they see the Nike swish, or the McDonald's "M", or the Apple symbol; just like they see the three pinnacles for Adidas.

A logo says what you're about. I'll cover branding in another chapter, but branding is basically saying what sets you apart. How do people remember who you are? And what are you really all about? Branding encapsulates who you are. It's a statement. For me it is "Super Human Being · Superhuman Voice." That's my branding. That is who I am. That's what I give. That's what people can expect of me. You'll want to have business cards and everything else reflect that.

Equipment! Don't cut corners here. Producers can hear right through shoddy equipment. You don't want to get a cheap USB Zingyou mic for $39.99 on Amazon. Just because it's going to arrive via Amazon Prime and you'll get it the next day or two days doesn't mean it's the best for you.

Good is always the worst enemy of best.

Don't get good. Get best. Spend a little extra to reach that higher tier of quality. Producers want to hear someone who will stand out from the herd…and get heard. They want someone who is showing that they've invested in their equipment, so producers can hear a Neumann TLM103 mic versus a Blue Yeti. They can hear the quality in an MKH416 over an AT2020; an NT1 over an SM7B.

Producers can hear the quality in your studio. You will shoot yourself in the foot if you're using a poor mic and untreated studio space, and poor plugins overdriving your audio. It's your job to be a cut above the rest. You don't want to go *under* the rest by cutting corners and getting cheap equipment, cheap free software that doesn't allow you to sound broadcast-ready. You can't make clean audio with an untreated sound space. Are you using a cheap USB mic and Audacity? It just doesn't work that way.

Invest in yourself. If you can afford one mic, buy the one just *above* it that's a little bit more expensive. If you can afford that, buy the one just above *that* that's a little bit more expensive. Push yourself to get a higher-tier, better-quality mic. There's a reason why these are expensive. You do get what you pay for. Push yourself to get good quality studio treatment of your acoustic space. Push yourself to get great software. That is what the big boys play with. Push yourself for things that you'll *need* for business.

You need stationery, you need business letterhead, you need something across the top of a Word document that says your name, your contact information etc. That stationery shows that you're a professional, it's not just a blank Word document with typed-in contact info.

You want a website? Sure, you can get something for free through Wix or Weebly or some other free software called WYSIWYG design ("What you see is what you get") where you just drag-and-drop in different elements. But you'll see at the bottom of all of those websites, "created by Wix", "created by Weebly", *whatever*, and then you're advertising *Wix or Weebly*; you're not advertising you. My website is supervoiceover.com: it is a WordPress-based website. And there are no other advertisements on there except for that I'm a WOVO member and a SourceConnect studio, or that it was designed by my web designer (he gets a designer credit). That's the way I want it. That's the way I need it. Keep them there. Don't give them any reason to be distracted.

Get a domain that is completely *your own* domain. And get an email address that has your domain in it. Why settle for free? For example, robsvoice@gmail.com, or suzysaysthings@gmail.com. Don't settle for those! Get your own personalized domain. And get suzy@suzysaysthings.com. Get rob@robsvoiceovers.com. Get a branded email to go with your website. It all looks so much more professional.

If you're looking for a great web designer that is low-cost, with excellent SEO-friendly design, check with Chris Cummings and IWD at chris@iwdonline.com, or Joe Davis with Voice Actor Websites[32].

Cognito forms are free forms that you can sign up for if you don't know how to create a contact form on your website. Perhaps the WordPress widgets don't work very well, or they're failing to reliably send you the results for some reason. You can go to Cognito forms online and create free plugin forms where you can simply grab the WordPress code and paste it into your website code. They work perfectly, fluidly, and they store all the results. They are excellent, free, and very customizable.

Definitely have a prominent Demos page, or a demos player on your website. I was counseled to have my demos on page *one*. Don't make producers go hunting for your demos. You want to have them front and center. You can have them hosted perhaps through SoundCloud or YouTube or wherever and then link to them through your site. But the less producers have to go searching for your excellent demos, the less they have to scroll, the more they'll stay with you, and the more they will not consider someone else. Have it all in one place.

There are contract templates out there that you can use. Check with lawyer and voiceover artist Robert Sciglimpaglia[33]. You can ask him what works and what is recommended (or not) to have in your contract. I also have contract templates available in my Super Voiceover Docs suite[34] that have standard clauses which protect your interests. Contracts are essential – they are *imperative* to protecting your interests. Now, if you're doing voiceovers on a site like Voices.com, or The Voice Realm (I don't recommend The Voice Realm at all, and you have to be really careful with Voices.com), then those marketplaces take care of the contracts for you.

But if clients are contracting you *directly* for voiceovers and you're not dealing with them directly through a middleman, you want a contract that has clauses that protect you and your interests. For example, for my first time international clients, I have them pay 50% upfront. If they don't pay 50% upfront, then their files have an audio watermark on them. And then after they've paid in full, then they get the release of their files without watermark. So, that way, they've paid in full; or they've at least paid their 50%.

Employ a "hold harmless" clause so clients have to hold you harmless. This protects you from legal responsibility in the event that something goes wrong with your recordings.

Employ a clause that says your net terms are payable by the net terms date stated, not "if it's 30 days net terms, you can pay by 45", etc. Employ clauses that ensure that you are paid, and not only paid, but paid on time. These clauses are so critical in running a business, to save you headaches.

There are ways to advertise when you're mobile. You can get custom apparel: I have all kinds of different shirts that say things about voiceovers - and people ask questions about them! I also have a vehicle that has vinyl lettering on the back window. Why not? What if I'm driving along and someone sees *"Need a Voiceover artist? Thatvoiceoverdude.com and 206.557.6690"*? If they happen to be a video producer, and I don't have vinyl lettering on my car, I've missed an opportunity right there on the highway. If there is a video producer who needs a voiceover artist and I'm driving by, I would rather have it on my vehicle than not. It also helps to deduct mileage and depreciation on your vehicle as a business expense, because you're using your vehicle for business. Get vinyl lettering. Believe in yourself. If you're a voice artist, tell people about it.

One invaluable tool that I've discovered not a lot of people take advantage of is a disposable phone number. I use the "Burner" app for iPhone. I have a subscription for three disposable phone numbers. If a call comes in on my phone, and it's a potential client, I know that they're calling Joshua Alexander, I know that they're calling in regards to business, that it's not just a personal call. I don't want to pick up my phone and say a casual "Hello?" if it's a client. If they're calling Joshua Alexander, I don't want to say "Hi, this is Josh." No. I want to say "Josh Alexander, may I help you?"

Burner is a great app to be able to help you determine which calls are business and which calls are personal. It's a marginal nominal subscription fee that you pay monthly or yearly. But it also protects your personal cell phone number so you're not throwing that out into cyberspace and then enabling everybody and their mother to have it. You might get a really nice vanity number that just sounds great! You don't want that out there in cyberspace; get a protective, masked disposable number that people will associate with you. You might even luck into a number with seven digits such as MYVOICE. You put *that* number on all your stationery, website, business cards, everything. That way it protects your personal cell.

Get a press kit and put it in a zipped file on your website. In that press kit, you can have all your demos, a glossy, a resume, your digital business card, etc.: you can have whatever you need to put in there that a client may want to download, and have everything they need to know in order to consider you. Sometimes producers and clients are just going a mile a minute, and they're skimming through voiceover websites. Maybe they go to yours and they say to themselves "I don't have time to listen to all of these right now." Then they see a downloadable press kit. *Bingo.* They hit the download button, save it to their laptop, and listen to it on their own time. That way you've made contact with them. You've provided them a convenient way for them to be able to review everything they need in order to consider you, and on their own time. You might not have missed out on an opportunity that way.

Uptime Robot[35] is a tool that I've used for my websites over the years. It's a free service. You program in your website. Anytime your site goes offline, Uptime Robot will email you. I want my sites to be online 24-7. It's unrealistic to expect that they will *never* go down, but I want them to be up as much as possible. I don't want people going to my site and seeing a 404 error. I don't want them seeing something that wards them away to the next voice talent. I want them to stay right on my site. Uptime Robot is a great tool to let me know if something is amiss with my hosting.

This next one is absolutely critical beyond any other tip. *You must have goals.* Invisible goals are no goals at all. You need a daily goals checklist. Email me at josh@supervoiceover.com: I'm happy to give you, for free, my Microsoft Excel goals checklist that I go by every day. A goals checklist will help you stay on top of your marketing, your other advertising, how many auditions you do, who you're talking to, etc. Did you reach out to marketing contacts today? Check. Are you working on a book? Check. Did you work on a chapter today? Check. Did you write your blog for the week? Check. It's totally customizable. You put your goals in there, and you track them on a daily, weekly, or monthly basis.

Make those SMART goals visible to you. You may have seen the acronym for SMART goals:

- S-pecific
- M-easurable
- A-chievable
- R-ealistic
- T-ime-bound

Have those goals visible so that you can actually see them and accomplish them; not some ethereal haze floating out there where you're thinking "what were my goals again?" No. You want to know what your goals are every day, all the time, so that you can keep track of them and accomplish them. Also, bonus! I once heard a *great* suggestion to add an -er to the end of your SMART goals.

Make them smart*ER*! Not just specific, measurable, achievable, realistic, and time bound but adding an -er on the end, and making them more *E*xciting and *R*ewarding. Why not have smartER goals?

I have goals that I track every single day. Some of them include contacting 150 people a day such as video producers, production companies, ad agencies, production/casting reps, etc., via LinkedIn, Instagram, Twitter, Vimeo, YouTube, etc., all the time, every day. If I'm not performing voiceovers, auditioning or blogging, then you'll find me marketing. I am a marketer first, and then I am a voiceover artist. That marketing is part and parcel of being a business owner. In order to put my service out there I need to market. Keep track of what you're doing with marketing. Make it a goal to market and fulfill tasks each day.

Another thing that I do every day is I post an interesting poster on Instagram. Now, when I first started doing that, they were memes or infographics. They were comical, incorporating lots of pop culture references, because I'm kind of a geek that way, and that's part of what makes me unique. Lately I've decided to just be a little bit more serious and be a little more encouraging. What I'm currently posting are professional VO tips or inspiring quotes. And every day I post one for the VO community-at-large. They focus on how to run a better business, or how to be a better voiceover talent. Those help the VO community! And that's also part of marketing, because if you use the right hashtags, your potential clients can see you doing that. Check out my Instagram channel @seattlevoiceoverartist for some examples of my posts.

A tool that I'm really fond of is the SearchTempest.com tool. SearchTempest is a site that will help you scour all of Craigslist in the jobs or gigs category. You basically search for *voiceover* or *voice talent* or *voice*, whatever. You can program variables so it will search for different strings on all of Craigslist, not just a single city - because you can do that on Craigslist itself easily enough.

SearchTempest will scour all of Craigslist, every city all over the planet for anything that is a voiceover job and return those results to you. I love SearchTempest because I can see all the results in one place and find jobs on Craigslist. They do exist! Some of them do not pay well; some of them do. SearchTempest is a great tool.

Another one of my goals every day is to follow five to ten voice talents or video producers on Twitter. I like building those associations. I like following people and seeing what they're up to in voiceovers. I also like following my clients, letting them know that I'm here, and conversing with them on social media. You can actually even score auditions by following the right people on Twitter who post castings.

Tracy Lindley, who runs the VO Edge, is very social on LinkedIn in particular. She posts engaging content that draws in clients and colleagues. You need to interact with those clients and be a *human* with them. Humans like humans! Have human contact with these people, and *engage* with them on social media. You do that by reading their stories, posting your own stories and asking questions, sharing articles, getting people to interact and engage with you. That's how you develop a following and an audience. And that's how people remember you and follow you. Don't be "that guy" who always has to talk in some grandiose put-on voiceover voice, pretending he's Don LeFontaine. It's shallow, it's an act, and it's repugnant. Be a real human.

Another of my goals every day is to work on my weekly blog. I usually release a new blog every Monday: they are inspirational, comical, and motivating to continue the voiceover journey.

People ask me often: "how do you have time to do all that marketing?" The answer is simple. I do not "have" time - I *make* time. Now, am I some almighty being who is capable of expanding our 24 hours into 28 per day? No. I neither have nor want such power.

In the 24 hours that *are* allotted to me, and the eight to ten that are allotted for work, specifically, *I* choose what I want to do with those hours; it's up to *me* to choose what to do with that time.

Ultimately, my job is to be able to put "irons in the fire" out there to feed that pipeline; to connect with clients; to keep things coming back to me. Everything I throw out there is a boomerang. I want those boomerangs to come loaded. I want them to bring back materials, clients, etc.

I want them to bring back contacts, interests, and communications. I want clients to say, "Sure, send me your demos." I want that to return to me a good return on investment (ROI).

For my efforts to make a return on investment, I want to get those marketing outreaches done every day. My business utterly depends on this.

So again - do I have time? No, I *make* time because I want my business to be a success. You need to adopt the same principle if you want your business to be a success, and really employ that marketing every day. Make time for it.

THE HUSTLE

I'm going to give you an acronym that has never been heard before. I made it myself. Soon this will be repeated everywhere and I'll be called *genius*.

It's called *hustle*. It's six letters, and I'm going to break it down for you. Hustle is so critical to your success not just in voiceovers, but in life.

Many times when I send out a marketing email to someone I've never talked to before, I've actually gotten a reply back that said, "Great work, Josh. I appreciate the hustle." I mean, *wow*! They've appreciated that I've contacted them. They appreciate that it is, in fact, a hustle: that I'm trying to get myself out there.

- The H stands for *hungry*. You have to stay hungry in order to put food on your table. You have to stay hungry for work. Keep that hunger - H is hungry.
- U is *undeterred*. The fact is that you're going to get some people that don't want you to contact them and say "take me off your list right now." You cannot be deterred by these people. They're just angry grumps, or they'e had a bad day. The next person, or the next-next-next person will inevitably say "thank you for emailing. Sure, I'll put you on my roster." Be undeterred in the face of resistance.
- S is *strategic*. Be strategic with your hustle. Don't just throw craziness all over the universe and hope that something sticks. Be *methodical*, be *systematic*, be *professional* in your hustle; be *strategic* in how you put your marketing out there with people. This also pertains to business as well. Be strategic in how you run your business.
- Be *tenacious*. Don't give up. This is an everyday a week thing. It's a 24/7 pursuit. This hustle is 24/7. Keep feeding that pipeline. Be tenacious with it.
- L - *living the dream*. You are living the dream in voiceovers. This is such a dream career! I pinch myself every day that I get to do this, and some days I wake up laughing. It is a *dream*. Live this dream that's part of your hustle.
- The E is *endless*; it never ends. You don't ever stop hustling in voiceovers; you don't just coast and rest on your laurels. It doesn't just kind of become this commission bounty, and

these royalties and residuals just stream in all over you. It's a constant hustle – endless – until Jesus returns. You have to develop a long-term vision in order to understand the endless nature of hustle, and sustain that vision.

OTHER TIPS

You may have heard of the concept of duplication: this goes back a little bit to coaching. You receive what others instruct, you learn it, and duplicate it. Why people want to reinvent the wheel is beyond me. You've heard the phrase "if it ain't broke, don't fix it." Duplication spares you from reinventing the wheel.

Follow those who have gone before, and adapt it to your own style, your own flavor, your own taste, but *duplicate* these people. There's a reason they're successful. This is really why you get coaching, and why you skip coaching to your own peril. These people have done it. These people are *doing* it.

Don't. Skip. Coaching.

Duplicate those people that are successful, emulate them, take what they do, do it for yourself. Duplication works. Take their chocolate-chip cookie recipe and, what the heck, maybe throw almonds in it. It's still a chocolate-chip cookie recipe that you duplicated and built upon. And *everyone* likes chocolate-chip cookies.

I never once saw voiceovers as a *hobby*. I never once treated it that way. When I discovered what I had, I *knew* this was it. It was always a business venture. For me, it made absolute sense because it makes use of all of my giftings: organization, empathy-giving, performance, business acumen, and more. I once wrote a blog called, "I'm a voice talent and I wear makeup."[36] It's all about the makeup that makes up who we are. Check that out in my blog; you'll find it humorous.

We all have different makeup. Some of us may underachieve in one area, or perhaps overachieve in another. Bottom line is: treat this like a business, never a hobby. Use all of your gifts. Look at this industry and this vocation, and say, "Is this making use of all of my gifts?" If so, you're going to succeed. If not, find out what gifts are that you might be lacking, and get training in order to *develop* those gifts. Build them up so that you can succeed and be well-rounded in this industry.

SUSTAINING A THRIVING VO BUSINESS

Now - how do we *sustain* a thriving VO business? How do we actually keep this thing called voiceovers going every day? How do we grease the wheel in order to see this continue to rotate and produce results and take us places? I'm going to go through a list here of just a bunch of different things, as before.

Ask for reviews from clients to form a Yelp page, a Google Local page, and/or a Facebook page. Reviews tell prospective clients that current or past clients liked you. Get reviews as often as you can, and everywhere you can. Be shameless about that. Try to recruit those reviews to build up your page and your reputation, so that people can find you on Google, Facebook, Yelp, LinkedIn, wherever. Recruit those endorsements and recommendations on LinkedIn. They're invaluable. Get those, because that's no longer *you* talking about how good you are. I hate tooting my own horn that way. It's other people doing that PR work for you! There's nothing better. A good word is better than great riches.

> *Don't ever guess what you should be making. Don't ever apologize for your rates. The rates are what the rates are, and the service costs what the service costs.*

Learn to say *no*. There are a lot of things that will come at you in your business, such as ways to try this or do that or help this person or that person, AKA, "get sidetracked." *No is your favorite Yes.* Learn to say no, because that's saying *yes* to you. Your time is your most valuable commodity. Don't let these "time sucks" come along and bleed you dry. There are people who are walking umbilical cords and they'll plug right into you and they'll just drain you dry. You don't want that - steer clear of that. Learn to say no to distractions i.e., too much scrolling through news feeds on social media, playing games like *Bejeweled,* and other distractions on your computer. There's marketing that you can do. There's learning that you can do. There's practice that you can do. There's research you can do. *No.*

The GVAA Rate Guide[37] is an excellent guide for what you should make in voiceovers, in case you're not familiar with it. It's pretty much the universally accepted rate guide for voice talent, and is probably the best and most well-known market rates guide out there. *Gravy for the Brain* has a good one as well. Voiceovers.com has a rate calculator that's called DeCypherVO[38]. The GVAA Rate Guide, however, is widely touted as the gold standard for rates. So if you're trying to figure out what you should be paid for a voiceover job, please don't guess! Go to the rate guide. It's got your answers right there for you. Ask questions, and you'll find that many voice talent who are established and vetted, who are booking work, etc., will corroborate that. Don't ever guess what you should be making. And don't *ever* apologize for your rates. The rates are what the rates are, and the service costs what the service costs.

Never overpromise and underdeliver. Do the opposite. I love Scotty (Mr. Scott) in Star Trek 3. Captain Kirk asked him about his repair estimate. Scotty said "it will take eight weeks, sir - but you don't have eight weeks so I'll do it for ya in two." And Kirk says "Mr. Scott, have you always multiplied your repair estimates by a factor of four?" And Scotty said, "of course! How else can I keep my reputation as a miracle worker?" I love that! Don't overpromise people; *under*-promise and *over*-deliver. Does that make sense? That way people are *pleasantly surprised* when you deliver quickly. They're surprised when you respond right away. Unfortunately, this is a huge trap that a lot of business owners fall prey to, because they want to get work - and I do understand that. Don't surrender to that mentality. Keep your wits about you. Underpromise, be rational, reasonable, and then overdeliver.

Don't obsess over whether you've been given a "thumbs up" or a star rating or "liked" on any of these P2P sites. If you get a four-star out of a five-star review, who cares? If you get a three-star, ask what you could have done better, if you're afforded that possibility. But if you ever get a no-response or a low response, don't hang your hat on that: you can't steer your life by the rearview mirror. You have to keep moving forward. Don't wait with baited breath over whether or not someone liked you. Don't stew over whether or not someone is going to get back to you on the role that you desperately wanted. You're better than that. Keep moving forward. Keep planting seeds.

I'm not going to go too heavily into this but if you don't have a smartphone, you're living in the past. Get a smartphone. You can use a voice memo recorder on your phone to help you record notes when you're out, and stay on top of things by checking the memos when you get home. Keyboard shortcuts on your phone save you *so* much time from typing the same exact thing over and over again. You can take notes when you're out, and remind yourself to take care of items when you arrive home, such as geo-fenced reminders. When I'm out getting groceries, I can ask Siri to "remind me to email Barbara when I get home and tell her 'thank you so much for the payment. And please let me know if I can work together again with you.'" Siri is great about that. And Alexa and other such devices, they're all great for keeping you on top of things like that.

Email signature: In your signature on your smartphone, you can put all your social media links and your website link. You want to direct potential clients to your website and demos, don't you?

Everywhere you can, as much as it depends on you, list your VO website for a quality backlink from whatever website you're on. If you're posting something in a forum somewhere, as long as you're not in violation of the rules, list your website, because Google will see that website pointing back to you. It's called a quality backlink. Google likes those.

KEEP UP THAT MARKETING

I'm going to talk about marketing at length in the chapter "Marketing & Visibility". But for a preview, know a few things as they pertain to business:

Marketing is not 80/20. It really is like 95/5. You're marketing *all the time*, every day. You have to develop a flavor, and a taste, and a penchant, and a *commitment* to that. If you're going to succeed as a voiceover business owner – or *any* business owner – you have to drive traffic to yourself.

You should follow up with your leads in marketing. You'll want to program Outlook or calendar reminders to follow up with them at regular intervals. Ask them how they're doing. Ask them did they get everything they needed? It's amazing how many times I've gotten a job simply because out of the blue, I asked how clients were doing right at that moment. That goes a really long way: reaching out to clients and saying, "How are you? How are you doing? Is everything okay?" "How are you doing?" goes a long way. And then you're back on their radar again, and they say "you know what? Josh really cares! I can tell he really cares about how I'm doing. I'm going to give him some more work." Love it! I love when they do that.

Is it manipulative? No. Do I genuinely care how my clients are doing? Yes. I have a client in Florida who was set to get married during in 2020, and then the pandemic happened. They called it off, not because they fell out of love with each other, but because it just wasn't the right timing. I care about her. She's brought me a lot of business, and she's a really good friend. Kathryn and I have had lots of great conversations about plenty of topics other than voiceovers.

These clients are your friends: many of them. So do what you need to do to treat them as friends and as human beings - and make sure tha they know you care. Send them gift cards. Send them holiday greeting cards. Thank them. Keep yourself on their radar by being involved in their lives. Your relationship with them doesn't have to be solely about voiceovers. Get to know their story too.

Marketing is so critical to putting bread on your table and continuing to share about your business. It's not something that everybody likes, I get it. But you have to do it if you want to survive as a business owner: you have to be willing to toot your own horn. You have to be willing to reach out and connect with people and tell them what you do. Vinyl lettering isn't enough. Wearing custom branded apparel isn't enough; having business cards isn't enough. You have to hand them out. You have to tell people who you are.

Mixers are a great way of marketing. Get out there! Meet people. Attend mixers with target-demographic business owners. Get out and meet those people! Tell them what you do. Have conversations, be real, be a human, talk about what you do and get the word out that way, while finding out more about them in the same stretch.

Again, I'll talk more fully about marketing later.

YOUR DAY TO DAY

Let's talk about daily structure. Make sure to structure your day clearly. Develop a plan of attack and settle into a routine. This again goes back to having a trackable goals system so that you can monitor your progress throughout the day, week, or month, and get into a system of marketing - and *adhere* to it every day. If you want to carve out an hour, a half hour, or even 15 minutes, make sure you have a daily schedule with reminders that pop up that tell you to do what you need to do. There's no shame in having these reminders. I've committed so much of my memory to my voice memo app, to my Outlook calendar, and to Siri, that I'm sure I'll end up with dementia and a bad case of drool. Ha! I've just done so much offloading of what I need to do that now it's all there to remind me, and I don't have to remember anymore. The computers and the technology are there for a reason. Use them, even if you'll end up a drooling freak by age 40.

If you don't blog, I want to ask why. Start blogging! It does not necessarily have to be about voiceovers; it can be about your life. Your blogs should be about 500 words minimum each – and content-rich. Google loves content-rich websites and blogs that have traffic to them, and where Google can recognize you as an *authority* on a subject. Google looks at me as an authority on the subject of voiceovers. Because I blog regularly, because I have traffic, because I have outbound links to other websites, and they link back to me in some cases, Google sees me as an authority. All search engines like sites that are active, and that have heavy content with keyword-rich blogs. They can be about whatever you want them to be. But they do show Google that you have an active site. Start blogging.

Reply *quickly*. Clients love it when they don't have to wait. Video producers are sometimes under the gun to get projects completed because you're the last thing that they need to drop in before they send it to their review team, or put it out there on the air. Clients love quick responses, and clients love quick auditions. They love getting answers to what they want. Don't you? Aren't we all the same? I don't know about you, but when I fire off a few inquiries to a contractor on Craigslist, the one who replies first is the one who gets my prime consideration; the one who replies week later and apologizes for their late reply won't even get a second thought from me; it's quite possible the job has already been done, anyway.

In the same light, your potential client didn't ask a question or post an audition casting so they could wait a few days, right? They need their answers now. The quicker you can reply, the better. I've been complimented here and there by clients who joked that they received an answer to their question *before* they even sent their question. Reply quickly, and impress your clients in so doing.

Get a customer relationship management (CRM) software! I actually created one, and it's Microsoft Access-based. If you have Microsoft Office with Access, then you'll be able to use this. It's called FirstVoiceData, and you can check it out at firstvoicedatacrm.com. It's specific to voice talent. It's cloud-based, so you can use it amongst a few different computers. For sending mass messages you can use an online CRM like Zoho, Nimble, Voiceoverview, MailChimp, and Salesforce - things like that. They're all paid subscriptions, whereas FirstVoiceData is not.

A CRM helps you keep tabs on your client base. You're harvesting leads out there, marketing, and those leads need to go into that CRM, so that you know who to follow up with. I've gotten jobs just by following up with clients who did not have any jobs the first time I contacted them. But because I followed up, I received the following reply: "Oh, you're right. Thanks for reminding me! I remember you. Yes! We actually do need a voiceover right now." It works. Follow up with those people. Put them in your CRM.

You should also have software such as an office suite: preferably, Microsoft Office or OpenOffice. These are all suites of software programs that you can use to put forward professional templates and documents, contracts, invoices, letterhead, anything that you need stationery for, anything that you need to send out to clients that has your contact info on it. You need something good, preferably something that you've invested in, that you can use to put forward a professional appearance. Plain text documents and in-email text-only proposals don't cut it anymore. Use office suites that help you *look* professional and *be* professional.

Digital organization: use logic! Use file folders and subfolders for your clients. If a client has booked you, make a folder. If they booked you again, then you need to separate their folder into two sub-folders. For example, Jake's Video has "Explainer Video" as a sub-folder. Now they're booking you for a national TV commercial, so you need two subfolders to keep those projects separate, in order to find everything when you need to. It is *critical* to remain organized. Organization is the BFF to a business owner. It's your best friend. Organization on your hard desktop of your desk, removing clutter, and organizing your Windows or MacOS desktop are important. Reduce the clutter in your life. Find your BFF.

I suggest using two different browsers: one for business, and one for personal. That way you don't convolute your messages. That way, you're not responding to a business client as a family member. That way, you're not posting something political, and one of your clients see it. That way, you're not bombarding your family with a bunch of advertisements and posts that deal with your business, rather than sharing foodies. I use Chrome in one monitor for my business, and I use Opera in another browser for my personal stuff. I keep that separation. That way I don't mix and match the two accidentally. Foodies and politics don't mix well with clients.

There are plenty of Facebook groups that you can join. I highly recommend joining the Global Voiceover Artists Network at www.gvoa.net: it's a great group. You can connect with myriad colleagues that way. There are several others. In the business of voiceovers, there are plenty of groups on Facebook, and LinkedIn as well. Learn from people who've gone before. Learn from people who are on the same career trajectory that you are on; ask questions; learn together. Grow together. These networking groups are indispensable, and there is no shortage in this day and age of online networking resources for us to be able to learn and grow together.

VoiceZam[39] is a tool I highly recommend - it's a plugin. You basically embed it right into your website. It has all of your demos in a little jukebox format. Interested prospective clients who go to your website don't have to scroll far. It's right there. They can go through a number of categories of demos that you provide! They can play them one by one, or download them.

Much like a press kit we talked about earlier, with VoiceZam, your clients can download demos to listen to later. Or, to add you to their talent pool. VoiceZam is $14 a month for their subscription service, which in my opinion is well worth it. It's an optimum, customizable player to have on your website. The reason why it's optimum is that it helps you track *listens:* it helps you track audience response and ROI on your marketing.

The way that I track if my marketing is working is if I actually look online, and see my *listens* going up. If I'm getting a bunch of listens, that means my marketing is working. That means people are seeing my email, responding to my email, going to my website, and playing my demos. VoiceZam tells you which demos were listened to, which were downloaded, how much of your demo was listened to, where the person is coming from, and what Internet Service Provider they use. It's an amazing tool, though a little creepy. But it does tell me a lot about my demographics and my ROI.

You're never done learning. The day you stop learning is the day you're room temperature…and the day you die. You always have to learn and grow, because trends change in the VO industry. Presentations change, marketing tactics change, tendencies change, and advertising styles change. The way you read changes. Please: *never stop learning.*

Return to coaching, return to groups, return to group teaching. It's just so critical. You have to continue to grow. I think the phrase was "grapes grow best in bunches." I'll talk about that a bit more here coming up. The more that you can associate with colleagues who can teach you, or with mentors who can teach you, then you're going to be a really rich, delicious, succulent grape. Or something.

Always be grateful. I started this chapter with that tone. Always proceed in gratitude. Never forget the first client who hired you.

Many times I'll return and I'll go back to Dale Peterson and I'll fire off an out-of-the-blue email such as, "Hey, I know that you're probably not thinking about me, but I was just thinking about you and wanted to say thank you again, for choosing me."

An out-of-the-blue email like that just shows such resounding residual gratitude that just doesn't stop. And clients are very grateful for your gratitude. So always be grateful. It's the wheels that make the world go round.

Good is always the worst enemy of best. Good is settling for. Best is striving towards the ultimate. Best is *alive*. It's functional. It's success-building. Choose best. Never settle for good, or for "good enough." Choose best. You *can* do this. You *can* do voiceovers as a career. Make *best* choices as you do it.

I highly encourage you to treat it like a business: to take the steps necessary to invest in your business, to learn to grow, to buy the right things, to get the coaching, to treat it like a business so that you actually have something tangible where you can look back and say, "I am *so* glad I never treated this like a hobby and shortchanged myself in the process."

One more time for good measure: You absolutely *can* do this as a solid business that provides for you and your family.

Ready? It's time to start.

CHAPTER 4:
MARKETING & VISIBILITY

YOU ARE A MARKETER

Marketing is a very strong passion of mine. I'm humbled to have a voice, this God-given voice, and this ability to articulate. We all have it! It is absolutely amazing what we get to do with this voice of ours and with this intellect of ours, and the abilities to dream, to market, to promote, to utterly believe in what we're doing. To make ourselves a success doing something we love. Marketing allows us to get that God-given gift out there.

Again, "find what you love to do, you'll never work a day in your life." It's so very true. I don't *work* a day in my life, because I love what I do.

Now let's talk about branding for a minute. We're going to talk about social media visibility – and in that, branding is very important. I read an incredible book by Celia Siegel entitled "Voiceover Achiever." It is all about marketing and branding, and it is a wonderful book. I highly recommend it.

I enjoyed the movie *Batman Begins* with Christian Bale. There's one scene where Christian Bale's Bruce Wayne is on a plane with Alfred The Butler, and he's says the following:

> *People need dramatic examples to shake them out of apathy and I can't do that as Bruce Wayne. As a man, I'm flesh and blood, I can be ignored, I can be destroyed; but as a symbol... as a symbol I can be incorruptible, I can be everlasting.*

I'd like to encourage you from the very start: stop being only a person. You are no longer just a person, you are now a *persona*. A persona is represented by a symbol.

When you start looking at yourself as a *persona*, then you start moving more into the territory of being like the Nike Swish, like the McDonald's "M", like the three pinnacles of Adidas, like the Apple logo. When you stop looking at yourself merely as a person and start looking at yourself as a *persona*, you become more of a contender in the voiceover sphere, in terms of teaching, in terms of marketing, in terms of not just participation, but really making a difference.

One of the reasons I chose my Superman or "superhero" theme, is because we're all superheroes - and it is such a team. It's very much a team effort for all of us to be a part of. Here's my logo:

My brand tagline says *Super human being · Superhuman voice.* I give a lot in the voiceover community, thus the first part of my branding:

- I run The Voices In My Head Blog.
- I run the Global Voiceover Artists Network on Facebook.
- I wrote a book series to encourage - I love to encourage! It just brings some laughter. It's a joy, and a fresh focus.
- I wrote this independent book.
- I teach for free in webinars and online conferences.
- I review colleagues' demos for free.
- I share marketing tips and goals worksheets with those who ask.
- I occasionally give my books and training courses away.
- I provide 20-minute voiceover video consults free of charge to aspiring voice talent all the time, to encourage you to know and to awaken to the knowledge that you can actually do this as a business.

The first part is the giving side of it. I want to be a reflection of the generosity that has been sown into me. The *superhuman voice* is because I have a dynamic and diverse voice, different accents, British, Australian, Caribbean, Mexican, old, young, different styles and timbers and cadences, etc., and I wanted to offer a wide palette of vocal range.

So that's where my tagline came from. And that makes me more of a persona. Like when people see the Nike swoosh and think of Nike, I want them to see my logo, which is my VO badge or shield from the chest, a superhero-type logo, and think "Oh hey, that's Joshua Alexander!" It's a name recognition thing. It's an image recognition. It's something that you want to leave people with that they will always remember.

For me, I'm marketing all day long. I'm turning over rocks. It's the thrill of the hunt. It's trying to find the next potential client and to really conduct that outreach all day long.

Marketing isn't for everyone. Not everyone likes it. I really do. In some respects, I have a very shameless approach towards getting my services out there. You do have to be shameless in the promotion of your business, for you to survive and to be a contender in the voiceover marketplace, to offer something of value, and help people to see that what you're offering is in fact *in*-valuable. It takes a bit of an aggressive edge to continue putting yourself out there.

I'd like to share a section from the first book that I wrote titled *Voiceovers: A Super Business · A Super Life.* It's from a chapter called "The Thrill of the Hunt." The section talks about how the marketing aspect is really about the hunt. Not so much the acquisition, but the hunt:

> The lioness stalks its prey with stealth. Slowly creeping through the tall reeds, it eyes its wildebeest prize, that great mound of juicy flesh...that succulent payoff. But ultimately, the lioness has something far greater in mind than the final meal. It's not the payoff, really. Rather, it's the moment the wildebeest becomes aware of her, muscles flex, joints spring into action, and the wildebeest blows out of there like a tornado, desperate to evade the predator. That is when life happens for the lioness... for the jaguar... for the cheetah... eyes widen as their prey takes off...*and the chase is on.*

I wrote that in my best movie trailer voice.

That's really what this is all about everyday: looking, looking, looking and finding someone - and then the connection! That's the fruit of your labors. And it's so wonderful.

But back to sowing those seeds. Remember, marketing cannot be just about the finish line. Marketing needs to be about the *love* of marketing, or you will burn out. It must be about tilling soil, it must be about planting seeds. It must be about reaching out. It must be about the joy of connecting. That's what marketing is about. Fred Bear said "A hunt based only on the trophies taken falls far short of what the ultimate goal should be." And I agree.

I love the phrase from Reinhold Eisner who ascended Mount Everest without supplemental oxygen in 1980. He was asked "why did you go up there to die?" He said "I didn't go up there to die. I went up there to *live*." Does marketing thrill you? If not, it's time you figure out how to make it do so.

If you adopt a new perspective, *yesterday*, post-haste, that you are not a voice talent; you are a *marketer* who just happens to do voiceovers, you will start to become incredibly successful. As with being a businessman first, I am also a marketer first, who just happens to do voiceovers. That's why I'm successful at marketing.

Here's an approach I'd like to share in terms of marketing in my approach with customers. I use the "Ask" Approach.

- A stands for "Allowing"
- S stands for "Sensitive"
- K stands for "Kind"

Allowing: in this day and age you're allowing your client to go about their day. I tend to prefer marketing via direct email. It's non-intrusive, it's not "in your face" like a phone call is. It's allowing them to answer on their time.

Sensitive is along the same wavelength but it's more about not shoving your goods and wares down their throat. Not coming across as the very best voice artist there ever was. *"I'm the best voice talent there is"* is arrogant. *Sensitive* is not about hubris or bravado. Go in sensitively, understanding that you are one of *many* who offer an invaluable service. Humility will open doors for you.

You also go in *Kindly*. Use manners. Use please and thank you. Be respectful. *Ask* if you can send your demo reel.

I like the *ASK* approach because all of it reflects humility.

All of it also reflects the ability to leave the ball in their court. No high pressure. I'm not a high-pressure sales guy. I like to just extend the invitation, and I pretty much leave it at that. I will follow up if they've asked me to do so. I like to back off and just let them make the decision in their own time.

Thomas Edison said that "genius is 1% inspiration and 99% perspiration." What a fantastic truth. You're going to be marketing a lot. Get ready to sweat a bit. Want to know how I sweat? I market to about 150 people per day; sometimes closer to 200 people. And I get asked very frequently. "How do you have time?" How do you even have time to market to all those people? I'm going to go back to Thomas Edison's phrase again: "I don't have time. I *make* time." Very different.

I just do it. I "Nike *Just do it*." I choose what my day is going to look like - *I* decide. I am in charge of my own destiny. This is my business. No one can force me to do something I don't want to do. I decide what to do with my time and my efforts and my energy and my inspiration. In my business as the business owner, I choose how to run my business. If I want my business to go on, to continue, then I'm going to market every day. I'm going to choose to reach out to people every day.

I cannot subsist on the P2Ps, or my agents, or repeat customers; I can't subsist on just those. I need irons in the fire. I need to cast a wide net. And because I need to, I *choose* to. *You* choose what your day looks like. The question is not "do I have the time or not?"

Here's a good example: I was asked to teach on marketing for the *OneVoice* conference in the middle of 2020's pandemic, with a four-year-old who was constantly bursting into my office for attention, and a one-year-old who wants his Dada. I'm constantly auditioning and marketing and blogging. And to top it off, we were moving to a new home in the midst of all this. So I ask you, did I not have time? No, I *made* the time. I don't have a calculator handy. But if you take 24 hours times seven, that's a lot of hours! (I'm right-brained. I'm creative, so I can't multiply, ha!) But that's a *lot* of hours that you can do a *lot* with in the span of a week. The choice is really up to you what you intend to do with it.

> *I choose what my day is going to look like - I decide. I am in charge of my own destiny. This is my business. No one can force me to do something I don't want to do. I decide what to do with my time and my efforts and my energy and my inspiration.*

It's been said "work smarter; not harder." I tend to disagree a little bit with that - you do want to get to a point where you're working smarter more than harder, sure. But why can't you work smarter *and* harder? Why can't you do both? I like to do a "smarter, harder" approach. Not everyone is going to do the amount of outreaches that I do per week. And I'm not going to do the amount of outreaches that some other people do. Some people out there might eclipse what I do. I am not as effective as some, and some are not as effective as me. However you slice it, be effective. Get to work.

Work smarter and harder. There's no reason why you can't do both. That's why I'm a success. I work smart. And I work hard smart. I incorporate goals and corporate tactics. I have a mission statement, I have a mantra, I am *intent* on what I'm going to do with my day.

You just do it, and you just go through with it. Don't waste your day playing games and surfing news feeds, all the while letting an entire eight hours - 480 valuable minutes - slip away from you. Maximize your day. Do that with a clear focus and goals.

So how do I actually get this done? I think after a while, just as you do with a smartphone, for example, you develop muscle memory, you flick here, you push this, you do that, you slide here, you move that over, you slide down, you develop muscle memory for a lot of things you do in your life.

Muscle memory is very important in marketing, particularly if you're going off of lists for emails, or performing the same task over and over in contacting new potential clients. Case in point: each day I will market to my approximately 150 people. Now, I am aware that there have been studies that show that you can market more effectively at a different time of the day, or specific days of the week. I tend to do more of a shotgun approach with my marketing and cast that wide net, because in some respects I believe it's a numbers game, and you have *chaos theory* at play.

What is chaos theory? Chaos is the science of surprises, of the nonlinear and the unpredictable. It teaches us to expect the unexpected.[40] Ultimately, all of our hard-conducted tests and surveys and analyses can fall flat and be subject to change. One year people can respond better on a Tuesday afternoon. The next it's Thursday morning. The next it's Sunday evening. It's relatively inconsistent. So, my solution to that is to be consistent in just doing it every day, around the same time.

I usually will market in the mid-morning and get all those done. I market one at a time. I don't do bulk "bcc" emails. I love to market via direct email. And I'll market via email through Instagram. I'll also do that via emails that come from directories, harvested emails from mailing lists that I will either assimilate myself, or I've purchased. I will customize each individual email. So, if the client's email is rick@mulliganmedia.com, I will say "Hi, Rick!" as opposed to "Hi there!" My message is customized to that person.

I know that when I get an email from someone that says "Hi there!" that that message is not personalized to me. It's not customized to me. They didn't take the time to reach out to *me* specifically. They are shotting off multiple emails rapid-fire and hoping for the best. It's untargeted. So, my muscle memory comes into play by copy > paste > change name > send…copy > paste > change name > send. Rinse and repeat. Changing their name makes it much more personalized.

It doesn't take me but probably an hour a day to do my 100 to 150 emails. So don't make marketing this great big scary beast and say, "I don't have time to do that." *Make* time. My 150 outreaches per day are spread across emails, LinkedIn, Instagram, and Twitter follows. For the emails specifically, I am actually reaching out to those people directly.

Again, maybe an hour a day. And if I'm working an eight-hour day, I still have seven whole hours to audition and to produce and to make money and to be successful. One hour per day of marketing has reaped incredible results for me.

Did you know blogging is a form of marketing? Do you blog? If not, can you start? I'm going to refer a lot of people – as I often fo – to Paul Strikwerda's blog, "Nethervoice." It has been an incredible inspiration to me. I love Paul's blog. There are other voice talent bloggers out there that I greatly draw from. Sumara Meers is one. Tom Dheere. J Michael Collins. Michael Apollo Lira. Jon Gardner. Gary Mason. Paul Douglass. Craig Williams. Kim Handysides. Jeffrey N. Baker. Ian Russell.

When you blog, you're sharing content that's very important to you that has a voiceover spin on it. But your blogging doesn't necessarily have to be about voiceovers; you can write about your life. I write about voiceovers and I put a very funny spin on it. If you haven't subscribed to The Voices In My Head Blog, do so at itsthevoicesinmyhead.com. You'll get your weekly dose of inspiration and comedy through the eyes of a voice talent.

Blogging doesn't just serve me, though. And it doesn't just serve my audience. Blogging serves my position and my standing with Google. I talked about this in the previous chapter. So, if you have a voiceover website, and all you have on there is a page with your "about" info with your demos, a contact page, etc., you should setup a blog on there, even if your blog is only going to be 500 words about your current day. It can be about marketing, it can be about your family, it can be about whatever. But it is Google seeing your voiceover website, active out there in cyberspace, putting out content – again, content is king. Get into the habit. It doesn't take very long.

I actually put a little bit more effort into my blogs than maybe the average person because I spend a whole week refining them. I intend them to be very Dave Barry-esque. Very Steven Wright, Dimitri Martin, Brian Regan, etc.. I include analogies, satirical dry humor and wit, because laughter is the best medicine. And if I can wrap up my voiceover message in some laughter, I'll have a better impact and better connection points. The only thing I love better than blogging about voiceovers is *producing* voiceovers.

I absolutely love the creative avenue of blogging. Start blogging.

You can use a tool like an email spider to gather leads. It's a program where you look online in, for example, a directory of video producers. You grab that URL, and program it into a spider. In my case, I use Email Extractor 6. I program the domain in there, run the search, and it goes to that website and pulls down all valid email addresses that I can use in order to market to those people. An email spider is excellent for harvesting emails of potential clients.

True, an email spider is a little bit controversial because I'm data mining, and some people don't like that. We live in an age where people want their privacy. I do understand that. But they are in a public directory online that I can easily harvest and contact them. Will all those emails be current and valid? Probably not. Many of them are, and I've gotten jobs by doing so. Google "email spider" or Email Extractor 6 as an example, and start grabbing free emails out there.

Now, don't try to run Email Extractor 6 on Craigslist, it will get you banned. Don't try to do it on LinkedIn, Craigslist, Shoots.video, Facebook, etc: it will get you banned. Don't try to do it on these mammoth organizations like LinkedIn, for example, which has approximately 600 million members in the US alone. It's a billion-dollar company. And they have anti-crawl code in their sites, and sentry bots that can detect when you're doing that and can get you banned. So be careful with sites with programs like that.

Another effective way to market to people is going through Instagram, and clicking on someone's profile after searching by hashtag for "#videoproducer", for example. Go into their profile and click the Contact button, if it's there. The contact button will pull up an email address that is free for you to use and email.

Here's an email tip. Be careful and wary of spam laws in your country. The CAN-SPAM Act of 2003 is highly applicable to your marketing. If you're doing a mass mailing, you need to have an opt-out option programmed in there. When I do mass market emails through Zoho, for example, it automatically includes an *unsubscribe* or opt-out link: you've got to have those in any marketing emails that you use, or you're in violation of anti-spam laws.

Every time you get a warm lead, you have to harvest that email and you have to store it. Keep that email and follow up with that person. One of the mistakes I made from LinkedIn early on was that I wasn't following up with all these connections that I was making. I finally began establishing some relationships with clients that I followed up with later on. I think my initial connection with them was several months, or even a year, prior. I now make it a point to keep them on my radar. I once got an E-Learning job with a client through LinkedIn who then gave me several E-Learning projects after that...*because I followed up!*

You will never stay on their radar. They need to stay on *your* radar always.

This has worked over direct email as well. I will just go down my email list and re-establish communication with some former clients and express something like, "hope everything's well, hope you guys are doing well, especially now in the midst of this pandemic, etc. - hope you're staying safe." They reply, "I am! Thank you so much for asking - wonderful to hear from you! Hey, you know what? Son of a gun I actually have a project for you right now." Out of the blue. That would have never happened had I not reached out.

You have to remember to reach out. Program Outlook or calendar reminders to follow up with them. Follow up with clients you've done work for at regular intervals.

Be thinking about your visibility. Paul Strikwerda says "Being outstanding doesn't make you stand out. If people don't know you exist, don't expect them to hire you. If you really want to play the trumpet professionally, you better learn how to toot your own horn."[41] This is where you learn to market both continuously *and* shamelessly.

You have to be able to come to a point where you are okay with tooting your own horn and promoting yourself regularly and shamelessly, because you're not promoting a product. Your product is *you*. You're promoting *you* to people. And there's a great amount of rejection possible when you put yourself out on the chopping block that way.

I want to be memorable. I want people to say "oh sure, I know who he is." Johnny Depp once said "one day the people that didn't believe in you will tell everyone how they met you". I love that phrase, because there are tons of people that you cross paths with in life. You want them to say something good about you.

Jobs are everywhere. We talked about the thrill of the hunt before. I love how I can go about my day out there in public and wear something that advertises with pride what I do. I was in Safeway the other day, and someone saw my shirt and asked me about voiceovers.

Now, you do have to walk a fine line between exposure and overexposure. And only you can determine how much you're putting yourself out there. You will see the amount – and the types – of responses that you receive for the posts that you create. So if your posts are entirely business-oriented, and there's not a shred of personal connection points in there for humans – if there are no connection points for people to wrap their heart around, you're probably going to be unfollowed, you're probably going to be muted, you're probably going to be disconnected from…and you have to be careful about that. You're walking a fine line, so you personalize your outreaches, and you personalize your emails to leads.

Be *social* on social media! That's what it was created for! Dale Carnegie once said "a person's name is to that person the sweetest and most important sound in any language."[42] It is amazing the amount of likes on *personal* content - video specifically - as opposed to static business images or ads that I place. People are humans, and they like connecting with humans. People like things real and genuine. This is why I don't like programs like Hootsuite, because it's not "in the moment". And it's not how I'm feeling right now. I don't use those programs that auto-post your content at specific times. It's not spontaneous that way. Imagine the impropriety of posting a business blurb, splash, ad, whatever, wherever, and it happens to send – *because you programmed it to do so* – right after a school shooting. You have to be really careful and really real and genuine with how, and where, and what you post on LinkedIn and elsewhere.

Do you get birthday reminders for contacts on LinkedIn? Wish people happy birthday! Wish them happy anniversary. Congratulate them on their new position - that is being social. That is being human! That is recognizing people.

How would you like to have a tractor beam? The truth is that you already do. If you're using hashtags out there on social media, you're using a tractor beam to draw people to you. Hashtags are magnets. They are tractor beams: they draw your audience to you by using the associated words that your target audience is using in order for them to find you. It is very wise and prudent to use hashtags. I've made a practice of doing that.

One of the ways that I maintain good visibility is I post my website in as many online places as I can where I can get a quality backlink. Some good examples are Alignable, LinkedIn, Twitter, Reddit, Quora, Jam-Pan, Doodeo, SoundCloud, Craigslist, etc.. I want Google to see these and say, "Hey, there's supervoiceover.com again! Oh, there they are *again!* Oh and there they are yet *again!*" And so I go, in quality and reputation, up Google's indexing. That's the way that SEO works. Google likes those links. News flash: it's called "the web" for a reason. Google likes good content, good traffic, your site being fully optimized and being really about what it says it's about: being content- and textually- rich. That's how you maintain good visibility.

The only 'person' I really need to see me before anyone else does is Google. If Google sees me, everyone else will start to see me.

Here's a case in point: Google likes Craigslist. You may not remember, but Google used to have a tool called PageRank. It was a little progress-meter bar in Chrome's shortcuts bar. It would measure from 1 to 10. Of course, Google had a 10 out of 10 rating, because, well, it's Google. Craigslist, I believe had a nine out of 10 at its peak. So, if you post on Craigslist, Google is going to index that too. And therefore you're going to be indexed not just in Craigslist, but also in Google, *because Google likes Craigslist.* One of the reasons for this is because Craigslist is almost purely textual in nature.

Perhaps you've never tried advertising on Craigslist, but I'd highly recommend it. It's $5 for an entire month for posting. I've posted approximately 15 ads at a time per month in the major Craigslist city markets across the U.S., and I've done that on more than a few occasions. $5 per month is great pricing and great exposure!

Also, Instagram and Facebook ads are low cost per click, and you can optimize with hashtags. Something to consider doing!

Now, far be it from me to promote visibility solely *online*. Join a Meetup! Visit meetup.com. If you're near a major metropolitan city, join that major metropolitan city's Meetup for voiceovers, if they have one. If they don't have one, create one! Voiceover Meetups are fantastic. In 2020, during the pandemic, you couldn't exactly get together monthly at restaurants and rub shoulders with fellow voice talent who are doing the same thing, but you could meet virtually online, and have webinars as well. Those are almost just as good.

You can't break bread with your colleagues like you can in a physical Meetup, but those meetups are wonderful visibility· you can connect with colleagues, learn together, and also get referrals that way.

They're also really good for mixers. You don't have to join a voiceover Meetup. You can join a business Meetup such as what I mentioned before like BNI, Bizbuilders, Chamber of Commerce, etc. Those groups are great to try out. You may not want to join with their annual membership premiums and their monthly fees for this and that, but you can at least meet people once or twice before they require that you become a member. Get your visibility and your reputation out there and have them potentially refer you to others. You even get a free breakfast sometimes!

I believe in potentials. I believe in possibilities - that is my superhero quality. I have an unquenchable belief in possibilities. All of these so far are about trying out possibilities.

Find what *your* superhero quality is. This may shock some people – I alluded to this earlier – but auditions are marketing tools too. If you're auditioning regularly, each one of those blessed auditions is a marketing tool. Every single one is a marketing tool for you to connect with potential clients. You might get cast, you might not. But you still made exposure, you've still made contact, you've still shown the world "I'm Joshua Alexander, this is who I am. This is what I sound like" …and they'll remember you. This is one of the reasons why I provide between 200 to 250 auditions per week. I've always believed that it is a numbers game. I get auditions from eight different agents, I get auditions from five different P2Ps. I get audition requests from repeat clients and new clients. I like doing them, because they keep me sharp, but also because they put me in front of clients. You have to look at auditions as marketing tools too, and putting your best foot forward on every level includes putting your best foot forward in auditions.

If you follow my Instagram channel @seattlevoiceoverartist, you'll note a lot of different images and infographics that are often pop-culture related, or something to do with my family or whatnot. And sometimes they have a humorous twist. I want those to be memorable. Post memorable and engaging content, and people will remember and engage with you.

YouTube and Vimeo are great avenues to maintain visibility and connect with people! If someone you've done work for has published a video of your finished work and voice on YouTube and Vimeo, *comment* on that video! Thank them for choosing you. Applaud them for a job well done! That way, people watch the video, and they see your comment below and say "oh hey, here's the narrator" - and then they have a convenient link to contact you by. Are you hijacking their comment thread in so doing? I don't think so. You're merely pointing out that you were the voiceover, and that you were proud to be part of it. I wouldn't call that hijacking. Mean what you say, and do it in a complimentary spirit. Also – ask if you can share these videos that you've seen your clients post. That way you get more exposure as well. And then you could potentially use those on your website in your portfolio.

Quora is another great site where you can ask and answer questions about voiceovers, whether posed by clients or by colleagues. It is yet another quality backlink that you can create in those postings, linking back to your website and content. Anytime you post anything anywhere, include your website and contact info in a signature when you can. It's so critical to do that. Get yourself *all* over the web. It's a bit creepy, but Google sees it almost everywhere, even in an email signature. I don't know how they do it – I don't want to know: it's creepy, but it's effective.

Once again, I cannot recommend VoiceZam highly enough. I know there are other tools that you can use, but I really appreciate VoiceZam's Zamtistics. I like having a player on my website that is essentially a jukebox for the client on the front end, but on the back end, it essentially helps me track my visibility and keep my finger on the pulse of my marketing. I'm a storyteller. I need to know if people are listening to me and if my stories are being told. VoiceZam tells me that for $14 a month with the "Zamtistics" add-on. It is a great tool, and very easy to implement on your site.

Contribute to your fellow voice actors. There are countless ways for you to connect with colleagues, to share what you've learned, and to learn from them; to dream together; to cast goals together; to show that it really is possible. You will only be a successful marketer and you'll want to increase your visibility and voiceovers, if a career in voiceovers puts a *fire* in your belly. If you don't have that fire, you won't want to market and you won't want to be that incredible success. I *live, breathe, eat, sleep,* and *drink* voiceovers. Ask my wife: they're my passion and my delight. I *love* what I do.

I'm really fortunate that I got to narrate nine books by my audiobook client Thibaut Meurisse. The first book that I narrated for him was titled *Upgrade Yourself*.[43] It was a game-changer for me. That book is absolutely fantastic. It is a Tony Robbins-esque personal motivation compendium. It really rocked my world. I was very grateful! I don't like to do audiobooks. God bless all of you who do audiobooks. I don't like to do them: they require way too much endurance that I just don't have. But I'm really glad that I was able to narrate his book, and then his subsequent books, because all of them have been highly encouraging and motivating.

I want to motivate you as a business owner to develop *hustle* right away. Remember my acronym from before. I am often applauded for the hustle that I have, not just by fellow voice talents, but also by clients that I reach out to who have actually said, "I appreciate your hustle. I admire your hustle. Good hustle," etc. I'm going fast. I'm working hard. I'm hustling to bring in bread to put on the table for my kids. So get that hustle, adapt it, own it. Make it part of your life in your approach for business, and you'll be successful.

WHICH ONE ARE YOU?

I want to outline the difference between hobbyists and business owners before we close this chapter out.

Hobbyists make hobby money. Maybe a bit of coffee money here and there. Business owners create revenue. Hobbyists are thinking it might be nice to have a bit of loose change. That name is not a coincidence. Business owners on the other hand are focused on building something that lasts; constructing something that has foundations for the long term.

This industry is far too good to think you can subsist on Fiverr or Just Say Spots or SpeedySpots or GigNewton or Casting Call Club or The Voice Realm and think you're "making it." You are missing out on the bigger picture by settling for one of them. There is far too much revenue to be generated in voiceovers, and each time you settle for less, you hurt us all because you are setting improper precedents in the minds of clients that they can get you on the cheap.

I'll quote Paul Strikwerda again: you don't want to attract "clients that expect a gourmet meal at a fast-food price and at drive-through speed."[44] You deserve more.

Lose the hobbyist and earn what you're worth!

Hobbyists have a pastime. It's an occasional fling. Business owners create an ecosystem. The former jump in every once in a while, subject to their emotions and whims; the latter erect a foundation that weathers time, economy, and more. It's building your home out of straw vs. bricks. There are only a few wise little pigs. Don't let the big bad wolf come blow down your hobbyist house of straw. This is not a leisurely activity that you pop in and out of. My voiceovers are 9am to 5pm Monday through Friday, just like a normal job. *Workin' 9 to 5, what a way to make a livin'…* Except *this* livin' is an utterly fantastic livin'. My voiceovers are done in a studio within an office, just like a normal career. They are growing and I'm moving up, just like a normal vocation.

Hobbyists dance around success; business owners *are* the success.

Hobbyists are a dime a dozen. They're the sheep. Business owners are one in a thousand. They're the shepherds. They're the pace-makers, the trendsetters, the goal-hitters.

Hobbyists follow along and aren't convinced that they need to take notes. "Give me a break, I'll remember this for sure." Meanwhile, business owners are scribbling detailed notes to refer back to.

Business owners take everything they've learned and assimilate it into a focused, tailored approach that is unique to their gifting and styles, enabling them to do what they know, and live how they can best grow in skill. They don't stagnate; they start producing, and people take notice. In the end, even chimpanzees have leaders that all the others follow.

Hobbyists have fly-by-night morality that depends entirely on what it will cost them. They don't see the need to obtain a business license because that means that they'll have to pay taxes on their hobby money. They see no need to get an LLC that will cover them in the event of a legal disagreement because of the one-time cost of $150, which seems insurmountable to them.

Business owners, on the other hand, happily register their business with local, state, and federal authorities because they want to be established, and they firmly believe that paying taxes is the right and ethical thing to do. Hobbyists hope no one notices and seek to stay under the radar. Business owners take great pride in knowing how much they've made and knowing that paying taxes is what is required of responsible citizens.

Hobbyists think that what they do is good enough; business owners, on the other hand, are never satisfied. It's never enough! They go the extra step…from marketing, to recording…to auditions. As Yuri and Tara say in *Voice-Over Voice Actor,* "You don't want to give them any excuses not to fall in love with you."[45] Hobbyists use excuses like "It was good enough." Business owners would never say that.

Hobbyists see no need for a logo, branding, or any symbol of who they are. Their identity isn't wrapped up in their craft yet; so, there is no need to adopt a symbol of their greatness or their skill. It's futile to pursue any kind of epitome of their offerings; they haven't arrived yet at a place where they see their vocation of monumental importance yet.

Business owners, on the other hand, see a logo and branding as utterly definitive of who they are, and what sets them apart. They are *self-aware*, and know that providing great service doesn't make them unique; providing great service that is absolutely a cut above the rest is what they strive toward, and *that* is what makes them unique. Concordantly it's easy for them to look at symbols and choose something that demonstrates the qualities that they already, or want to, showcase. Lao-Tzu said, "When you are content to be simply yourself and don't compare or compete, everybody will respect you." Be utterly yourself. Be utterly even *more* than yourself.

Hobbyists look sadly at every cost, and wish that life didn't exact so much from them. Sometimes they're even looking for a handout. Business owners, on the other hand, look at expenses as *investments*. The problem hobbyists have with expenses is that they lack patience: they don't grasp that it first requires a willingness to plant a seed before you can watch it grow and enjoy its fruit. *They want the fruit, not the growth*. And sometimes, like Queen sang, they want it *all*, and they want it *now*.

Any good thing worth pursuing takes investment. Business owners who have skin in the game know that their investment can pay back dividends. The pride a business owner feels when they own something outright and bought it with their hard-earned dollars far outweighs the joy the hobbyist feels when they've been given a handout.

The business owner feels gratification. The hobbyist feels relief. That relief, once put into words, would sound like "Phew! Dodged a bullet there. Almost had to spend some money!"

The business owner can successfully say "*I* did this. No one else. *Me*."

The hobbyist uses everything free and hopes that a producer will like the substandard product they churn out with all their free goods: Wix/Weebly, Audacity, $39 mics on Amazon, cheap headphones, USB mics, and discounted computer speakers. Then they get mad and jealous of all those around them who are succeeding. They wonder why it's not fair, and they shake their fist at the world.

I know of one such aspiring voice guy who I gave a *free* consult to that got everything for free and was expecting to succeed. The next post I saw from him he was asking his Facebook friends to give Christmas gifts to his son because he couldn't afford it.

Skin in the game.

Hobbyists have simple email agreements and handshake deals. Business owners seal their deals in blood, with contracts that contain clauses that protect their interests.

Hobbyists throw their finished audio out there and hope to be paid in a timely fashion, with no recourse if they're not. Business owners' contracts contain net terms with defined grace periods and 1% daily late fees.

Hobbyists go for the one-and-done approach with their "clients." They're grateful for that one payoff and then goodness knows if they'll ever see that client again. Business owners develop long-lasting *relationships* intent on future work.

Hobbyists hope their clients come back. Business owners *intend* for their clients to come back.

Hobbyists don't feel the necessity to create structure or anything that guarantees them a real shot at success. It's not a system for them; it's a random happenstance occurrence of maybes and hopes and what-ifs.

Business owners don't work that way: they don't *wait* for their dreams to come true; they *make* their dreams come true through concrete and comprehensive goal tracking and intention.

Remember, intention trounces hope every single time.

Hobbyists have fragile and limited payment avenues. They'll take PayPal and maybe Venmo. Even better, they'll just take straight under-the-table cash. Why report that to the IRS? Business owners provide their clients ease of payment, with multiple possibilities.

Business owners know that big clients who pay big bucks work on net terms and issue checks or pay via ACH or direct deposit: all trackable income that hobbyists don't like.

A hobbyist rents studio time. A business demands a home studio. If you're relying on a studio's availability for your every audition and your every recorded job, it's going to cost you, as Yuri Lowenthal and Tara Platt say: "Now, obviously, this comes at a cost, and won't be as flexible as having your own recording equipment."[46]

Hobbyists will unwisely, repeatedly shell out bucks to rent studio time in the short term; business owners will purchase or construct a home studio for the long term.

Here's the most important one. Hobbyists undervalue themselves. They'll allow themselves to be taken advantage of because they don't know the immeasurable value of their own service.

Business owners charge what they're worth. They have a firmly ingrained sense of deserving market rates, and charging rates commensurate not with their length of experience, but rather commensurate with what the service simply costs. It's not based on how long they've been in business, if the economy is on a downturn, do they need something on their resume, or feeling they somehow don't deserve it.

Business owners know the worth of their service, and they charge accordingly.

Hobbyists will charge well under market value out of desperation and wanting badly just to list some "big name" client on their resumé. They have no idea that many clients on the paying end are well aware of what a voiceover artist should make, and when the client see the paltry rates that the "voice talent" is charging, they know instantly that they're a novice; that they're not a team player; that they're desperate; that they can be taken advantage of.

These are not the clients you or I want, so why on earth would you be the voice talent that such clients want?

A business owner knows that the service costs what the service costs...period, end of story.

INVISIBLE GOALS ARE NO GOALS AT ALL

If you wander aimlessly through your day, if you're kind of hoping and praying that this day turns out well and that you're a moderate success on some level, that's not a goal. Have concrete SMART goals like we talked about earlier.

Go off of a checklist daily to ensure you're progressing towards an end goal. I'll remind you: please feel free to email me at josh@supervoiceover.com for a free goals worksheet - I'm happy to share that with you. You can customize it to your heart's content. This is important. You cannot hit what you cannot see.

There's a verse in Proverbs that says "go to the ant you sluggard", reprimanding the sluggard for being lazy and encouraging them to look at the ant: it's harvesting. It's preparing all its food, it's storing up for winter. Smart little animal! Be that smart little animal: ask for reviews from clients, form a Yelp page, a Facebook page and a Google Local page. Google sees those and sees active reviews being posted on an active account with a website linking back to you.

One of my daily goals is to spend 10 minutes thinking of what else I can do to benefit both the VO community and my own business. I don't do that every day. But that is one of my goals. What can I do to offer substantive content, to offer encouragement to help my colleagues grow? Again, I've been given a lot.

Once more, I have to come back to this. Try to look at purchases as *investments*, not expenses. This is a huge difference in perspective, as a business owner who wants to dream their business into reality. Every single penny you spend in voiceovers is an *investment* into your success. It is not an expense. And the sooner you get away from that perspective, the sooner you'll see a membership to a P2P as no big deal. The sooner you'll see vinyl lettering on your car (the purchase of it) no big deal. The sooner you'll see a hat with branding on it as no big deal. The sooner you'll see a StudioBricks as no big deal. Yes, they take a little bit of funding from you. But they allow you to *make* a lot of funding.

> *Proverbs 29:18 says "Where there is no vision the people perish." Make sure you have vision going forward. Be on sentry, keep your eyes peeled, turn over rocks as often as – and wherever – you can, because clients are out there.*

Most importantly, dream. This is not rigor. This is an incredible career that allows you to have fun, to produce, to be chosen. There's something wonderful about being chosen. When you're chosen to voice some fortune 500 company's script and be their brand ambassador, it's *huge!* Dream this business true by treating it like a business.

Always dream of how you can improve. Always envision upgrading yourself.

Proverbs 29:18 says "Where there is no vision, the people perish." Make sure you have vision going forward. Be on sentry, keep your eyes peeled, turn over rocks as often as – and wherever – you can, because clients are out there. They *are* out there, and the jobs *are* out there as well.

Vision sees things into focus. And remember:

Your focus determines your reality.

CHAPTER 5:
NETWORKING &
REFINING

GRAPES GROW BEST IN BUNCHES

We've talked about creating and sustaining a thriving VO business. We've talked about marketing and visibility as well.

Now it's time to continue that growth, to expand *outwards*, to connect with colleagues, and to talk about something that's so critical to refining your craft – and that's coaching. I cannot even begin to stress how essential coaching is. But I'm sure going to try. The hubris of the newbie says, "How hard can this be?" Let me tell you now: it's hard. You need coaching. You don't just pick up a mic and magic happens and all your wildest dreams come true. This is not Oz.

Before we discuss coaching, however, let's talk about another component that's critical for you. It's called *networking*. You may have heard the phrase before: "grapes grow best in bunches." It's very true! There are lots of communities online today that you can join. And you, as a grape, can join your fellow grapes and grow well together. There's a sweetness to be found in clusters. There's a sweetness to be found in these thriving communities where you can actually

> *"Success isn't about how much money you make. It's about the difference you make in people's lives."*

connect with colleagues, see who is on the same career trajectory that you're on, bounce ideas off them, ask about hardware, software, conferences, coaching plugins, books, resources, programs, whatever, and receive valuable feedback from those who have gone before you. You don't know it all yet. You probably never will. I recently wrote a blog about this, about how we're never really done learning, and when we are, we rot.[47]

As I discussed in a previous chapter, it's important to duplicate, it's important to receive feedback: *honest* feedback from people who have gone before, who have been down the road that you are setting out upon, and to learn from them. There is nothing more valuable or formative than that for your voiceover business.

Grapes grow best in bunches. Be a grape, and be part of the bunches of the grapes around you.

There are a few quotes that I wanted to share with you as we kick off this chapter. The first one is by Zig Ziglar:

> *"You can have everything in life you want, if you will just help enough other people get what they want."*

How's that for making sure to connect with others, to put their needs before your own, and to look out for your fellow man?

Michelle Obama also says:

> *"Success isn't about how much money you make. It's about the difference you make in people's lives."*

Love that one. We talked about networking before, but you can have all the success that you want and still be a complete island unto yourself. You can be completely cellular - insulated in your own little world. If you stay that way, you end up as Gollum. Don't be Gollum.

It's so important that we get out of our own little bubble and rub shoulders with those who are trying just as hard as we are, who are succeeding just as well (or not as well) as we are and learn from them together. It doesn't do you any good to be a Lone Ranger. Even he needed his Tonto. There are Tonto's out there that want to give. There are people out there that need to receive - and you have been qualified to give and receive from birth.

I love the quote by MiSha. She says, *"Networking is not collecting contacts. Networking is about planting relations."*[48] How true is that? It's about planting seeds, watering them and ensuring that they grow.

I want to tell a little story about how I got started really going full bore into voiceovers. I reached out to an old friend of mine in high school. I knew that he was in voiceovers, but lost touch with him and his family. But I knew through the grapevine – *there's grapes again!* – that he was doing voiceovers. So, I went to Google, went to his website, contacted him and said, "Hey, I'm thinking about finally launching full-time into voiceovers. I was wondering if you could help me with any advice or tips." And he wrote back and said, essentially, "Good to hear from you...talk to Scott Burns."

Wait what?

That was it! It was like two sentences. Just that little bit of brevity. And then he was gone. It was the strangest and most blessed thing, in the long run. Right then and there, I remember thinking, "uh... okay, I don't *know* Scott Burns. I know *you*; may I talk to *you* please?" It was so interesting – and a little discouraging from the very start – to be farmed out right away. I had been outsourced, or *offloaded* perhaps is a better word. But boy did fortune strike in that moment, because I found out quickly who Scott Burns was.

I will never forget sending him an email that was very brief, and getting a reply back from him that was *mammoth*. And it wasn't a mail merge email; it wasn't "Hi NAME...nice to meet you NAME...it's good that you're interested in voiceovers, NAME... allow me to help you, NAME..." No. It was all personalized. It contained personal answers to my personal questions, and he just gave and gave and gave - the man is a fantastic mammal. He is a walking exclamation mark, and if I leave my wife for anybody, it will be for Scott Burns.

Honey, if you're reading this, we're together forever, and Rick Astley and all of that stuff, so don't worry.

Scott Burns is a wonderful man. He's very generous, and I'm so fortunate to have him as my coach. Giving to others is not everyone's bag, I get that. Not everyone has the same *generosity* streak. Scott is a tremendously generous individual, and he comes to epitomize for me what is really *beautiful* about the voiceover community: that so many people are so willing to give, so many people are so willing to help. You are their competitor of sorts, and yet they're still willing to help you. That's a beautiful thing. It's a *wonderful* thing.

You're joining a community full of lots of people like that who give to others, review their demos, answer their questions, point them in the right direction, etc. They want to share your own experiences, share your successes and your failures.

It is so important to be absolutely honest as far as where you've been in the journey, and this helps someone else avoid pitfalls and roadblocks and canyons to fall into. We're not all lemmings here;

we're pursuing a common goal. And we want to help each other not fly off of a cliff.

Here's where Meetup comes into play again. You can network with colleagues through a Meetup in your nearest metropolitan city, or connect with your colleagues online virtually. It's great because you can get together monthly at dinners, break bread with colleagues, talk to people sitting across from you, learn from their mistakes, share ideas, ask questions, find out what works for them, and apply it to your own life.

The meetups and mixers are all excellent community-based organizations that allow you to connect with colleagues and really ask those important questions to learn, grow and rub shoulders with greatness. In so doing, greatness can rub shoulders with you, *and rub off on you*. You learn from those who have gone before. I take great pride in knowing and calling some bigwigs in the VO industry my friends. Scott Burns, Pat Fraley, Paul Strkwerda, Kay Bess, J Michael Collins, Gregg Berger, Tim Tippets and so many more. These are people that I consider role models. I'm very grateful to call them friends and to learn from them.

So, get out there! Commiserate with your colleagues, learn from them, teach them, grow together. Grapes grow best in bunches.

Another way you can connect is by joining group coaching. For example, J Michael Collins does group coaching now and then through agents, and you can sign up for those and do the "Brady Bunch" Zoom-style lineup of all of you in a grid, read specific scripts that you've brought, and receive feedback, praise, critiques, etc. You receive what you need to hear in order to perfect your craft.

Those are wonderful sessions to be a part of. There are also groups such as The Mic Check VO Workout[49] that you can join that do that on a weekly basis. Plenty of other groups conduct similar activities online.

We live in an era right now where there are far too many resources available to us online for us to actually fail. The resources are infinite; they are immeasurable. You can look online and simply Google "voiceover group", and you'd be shocked to find the sheer plethora of resources that are available to us to learn and grow together. They are on Reddit, Quora, Facebook, LinkedIn, Meetup, Clubhouse, direct websites like VO Peeps, The Voiceover Collective, The Voiecover Network, WOVO, Mid-Atlantic VO, Gravy for the Brain, and more. It's amazing.

Participate in those Facebook groups, those LinkedIn groups, those Reddit groups or any other groups that are of benefit to you. Get in there and give and receive, learn and impart, converse and participate. There are *so* many resources to help you grow.

I simply don't know how people way back in the dark ages of voiceovers in the late 60s did it; when it really came to prominence. The support community that we have now is just magnanimous and phenomenal. So please don't be an island unto yourself. Get out there.

Ray Kroc, the founder of McDonald's said, *"When you're green, you're growing, when you're ripe, you rot."* And how true that statement is! It is imperative for us as voice talent to continue learning. You're never done learning until you're you're pushing up daisies. We're all on a constant journey together of learning trends, seeing delivery styles change, things going in and out of vogue, adapting to change, rolling with the punches etc, in terms of assimilating new trends.

In 2020, there was "conversational", and then there was "parental and reassuring and paternal-type" voices to give encouragement in the midst of the pandemic. These trends change, and they vary, obviously, between genres of voiceovers, but they can also endure a quantum shift in how you're supposed to deliver your voiceovers through the years. So, continue to learn. Be adaptable. A rolling stone gathers no moss.

This is an industry where you're in great need of rejuvenation, affirmation, and encouragement. In the midst of the depression and frustration that you can endure by virtue of constant marketing and constant auditioning, we face a lot of rejection in this industry. As an entrepreneur, you face rejection anyway. But we face a lot of it in this industry in particular, through all the marketing and auditioning we're constantly putting out. Moreover, you need shots in the arm in order to get that replenishment of energy and affirmation to keep you going. It's very crucial in this industry to rub shoulders with people that can give you that shot in the arm.

A PERPETUAL EVOLUTION

Let's talk about coaching. I am not a coach, nor am I about to sell you a coaching package. Have I considered it? Yes. But with everything else I do, I don't really have it in me and I don't really have the time. I'm much more a mentor and an encourager as well as an auditioner and marketer. I'm the guy on the sidelines, with the pom-poms going *rah rah, you can do this*. I've foregone the spandex, of course, so don't worry. But I want to be on the sidelines being an encouragement to you!

There are a lot of people that migrate to the voiceover industry, because they were told they have a great voice. I have had that said to me exactly zero hundred and zero times. I don't remember, to ever having been told that. One more time: I'm a businessman who *happens* to do voiceovers. I just happen to be great at them.

> *"The key is not the will to win. Everybody has that. It is the will to prepare to win. That is important."*

But many people come into this industry assuming that it's easy.

I'm appalled when I talk to a newbie, and the subject of coaching comes up, and they brush it off. Their hubris gets in the way and they say, "Oh, I don't need coaching. I mean, how hard can this really be, right? I really don't need coaching."

Rookies do that to their utter peril. Coaching is part of the fundamentals of voiceovers. It's your first – and potentially your *only* – investment in voiceovers. Not everyone who gets into voiceovers should be doing voiceovers, and it's a coach's job not to lick your fingers and tell you things that you want to hear. It's their job to tell you one of three things:

    A.   you got it (meaning don't pay me anymore because there's nothing I can ethically charge you to teach you)
    B.   you don't got it (meaning don't spend a dime in voiceovers because it ain't gonna happen)
    C.   you don't got it, but here's how you get it (meaning let's talk about a roadmap to success for you, which will require some investment of course)

It's a coach's job to drop you if you are uncoachable - not to keep taking your money. It's also their job to drop you if you're already there, if you're already ready to deliver these scripts compellingly, and not keep taking your money.

I'd like to share a few quotes with you about coaching, and the importance thereof. These come from well-known coaches and motivational speakers.

John Wooden says "a good coach can change a game; a *great* coach can change a life." (italics mine)

Timothy Galloway says "Coaching is unlocking a person's potential to maximize their own performance. It is helping them to *learn* rather than teaching them." You've heard the phrase "you can give a man a fish and feed him for a day, or you can *teach* a man to fish and feed him for a lifetime."

Bobby Knight, coach, says "the key is not the will to win. Everybody has that. It is the will to *prepare* to win. That is important."

I absolutely love this last phrase!!! It is the will to *prepare*. So many people gravitate to voiceovers because it "looks fun." It looks neat. *How hard can it be?* And they just want to get in front of a mic and hit the ground running, so to speak, and try to churn out good quality material. They're using a Blue Yeti USB mic and Audacity, or they're using their iPhone Voice Recorder and recording that way. This is *not* the way to succeed. How many of their competitors *have* invested time and money and resources into obtaining quality coaching, equipment, software, and resources? Do they honestly think they stand a chance at being heard?

In my humble view, there are five important purposes a coach has.

Coaching is designed to help you:

1. determine the true meaning of the script, to get underneath the words, to really figure out what they're trying to say, and how you can express that well
2. get under those words and "lift" them off the page
3. breathe life into that script, to make it come alive, so that they are no longer just words on a page
4. *so* believe what you're reading that your *audience* believes you too
5. learn from them, and from their experiences, so that you can duplicate them.

Now, there are definite differences between a good coach and a bad coach. A good coach will be able to bring out the best in you; they'll be able to determine where your 'money' voice is, and where your signature sound is.

Also, a good coach can help you figure out where that voice is going to be the most marketable, to help you find the most successful genre to enter into. You might think you have a great voice for Character/Animation work. And your coach may say "No, no! Your voice is actually perfectly suited for E-Learning; you have a nice calming instructional voice that people would want to listen to. I could listen to you talk about vacuum cleaner assembly all day. I think you should pursue E-Learning."

A coach should be able to produce a competitive demo for you – a demo that's going to *wow* people, which will help you stand out. A demo that will help you be a cut above the rest. A demo that people will want to listen to and say, "Wow, listen to this guy! Just *listen* to this guy, would ya?" It's the coach's job to make a demo that is truly superb.

A good coach will be able to keep in touch with you and monitor your progress. A good coach will want to follow up with you on occasion; a good coach will *remember* you and be *proud* of you.

And finally, most importantly, a good coach will *not* take credit for your success. A good coach is there to help *you* be great, and to actually *exceed* them. A good coach is there to pass on what they've learned, and enable you to be incredibly successful. They will not take credit for your success; they will truly enjoy watching you soar.

Now let's talk about a bad coach for a second. Unfortunately, in many industries – the voiceover industry notwithstanding – there exists many a "coach" that is not meant to be a coach; such people are, in fact, predators.

They'll make many promises. They sometimes have expensive coaching bundles or packages. It's someone who usually knows just enough to make them *dangerous*. They think they have all the answers by spending a little bit of time in the voiceover industry in soaking up what they've learned. And so they pass it on, and they want to charge for it. But they're not the people who will sit with you beyond the confines of your pre arranged time, i.e., you have a coaching session from 3pm to 4pm, and they're firm about finishing it right on the dot. Once I was in coaching with Scott Burns, my coach. It was 4:15pm. We were scheduled to finish at 4pm. He asked me excitedly "you're doing great! Wanna keep going?" And out of respect for him I said, "Oh, no, no, it's fine. I appreciate it! We've had our hour!" Scott didn't care what time it was.

Conversely, a bad coach will want to cut you off as soon as they can, and get back to what they were doing. They don't have a vested or genuine interest in seeing you succeed. Scott wanted to continue well past the time frame.

I recently had a "run-in" with someone who has been doing voiceovers for less than a year and is already 'coaching.' They are putting out horrible amounts of misinformation and endorsing all kinds of incorrect and substandard equipment and relationships… they are leading people astray. It's maddening to see this. The only consolation is that they are receiving *plenty* of blowback from seasoned professionals calling them on the carpet.

And let me tell you about even one more bad example. There was another individual I knew who wanted to get into coaching. I heard from three individuals who sent demo files to her, requesting that this 'coach' review them. She had offered to review them! I'm told those people never received replies from that 'coach'. "Yes, send me your demo, I'll be glad to review and give you feedback!" Crickets.

These people never once heard back from her, presumably because they hadn't paid a cent to her. Such a 'coach' didn't have their best interests at heart, and doesn't ultimately care. Additionally, her background did not include voiceovers! It was from a radio DJ background, and yet she felt she could coach voiceovers, even though they she was just entering the field. Voiceovers and DJ'ing? *Very* different.

There's a phrase that I heard from my coach once, and it's pretty funny! It is as follows: "It's been said that those who can't do voiceovers *teach* voiceovers, and those who can't teach…teach *shop*."

I'm going to mention again what Dr. Ian Malcolm in Jurassic Park said: "your people were so preoccupied with whether or not they *could* that they didn't stop to think if they *should*." That phrase comes to epitomize bad coaches. Bad coaches are so preoccupied with whether or not they could, that they don't stop to think if they should. Someone who has what it takes to be a good coach will honestly *question* whether or not they would make a good coach. Why? They obviously are too humble to jump into that role – they want to make sure they're ready first. A good coach will know if they should be coaching. And on the learner's side, as the Bible says, "A tree is known by its fruit."

One of the ways that you can really determine if any coach is the coach for you is to *vet* them. This is why Facebook groups, LinkedIn groups, Reddit groups, etc, are so important for you as a budding voiceover talent. They're also good for one who wants to go back to the drawing board and perhaps relearn the essentials from a coach within the VO community.

Now, Scott Burns, he's the first North American voice of Bowser in Super Mario Brothers. He is an accomplished coach who's produced several demos for myself and well-known colleagues. Scott *is* vetted by the VO community, and he's known and respected. He's been doing it for a very long time.

Pat Fraley[50] is also a fabulous voiceover coach. He's not a demo producer, but he is very well known in the VO industry. On a side note, he gives *incredible* workshops! As the toy store version of Buzz Lightyear in Toy Story 2, Krang in Teenage Mutant Ninja Turtles, etc; just go to Wikipedia and and search for Pat Fraley on there. You won't have time to read his resume. It's extensive and amazing.

Here are some other great coaches who are all industry-vetted:

- Marc Graue[51]
- Elaine Clark[52]
- J Michael Collins[53]
- Everett Oliver[54]
- Kay Bess[55]
- Roy Yokelson[56]
- Marc Cashman[57]
- Dave Fennoy[58]
- Julie Williams[59]
- Bob Bergen[60]
- Anne Ganguzza[61]

There's a long list of greats. This little list doesn't even come close to incorporating everyone.

These coaches are vetted by the VO community: that should tell you enough to know that this person is trusted. Trust is a huge thing in the VO community as far as learning from those people who've gone before. If you can't trust them and what they're offering you, then you can't really expect to take their ball and run with it nor be successful. Again, you're *duplicating* a coach. If you're duplicating a crappy coach, you're going to produce crappy results, and you're going to receive (and put out) crappy information. And sometimes there are coaches out there that are labeled serial purveyors of bad information, because they perpetually misinform.

You have to be really careful in who you choose as a coach, and learn the correct methods for approaching voiceovers. Your very first expense in voiceovers could potentially be your very *last* expense. Coaching could potentially save you thousands and thousands of dollars, on hardware, in particular, and at conferences. They save you money by being honest with you if, in fact, you simply don't – and *won't* – "have it." Some people think they have it, and they are convinced that they should be doing voiceovers, when they just simply shouldn't at all…and they beat their head against the wall vainly and futily. A sound coach can spare them that agony.

A coach's job isn't just to direct you to the best hardware and/or software. It's to help you really bring scripts to life so that you will get repeatedly cast.

Here's an example. I don't like cats. My wife has a cat. We have a running joke that "we live at our home…with our dog…and her cat." But I don't really like cats. If I am auditioning for a commercial for cat food or kitty litter or something like that, I need to *sound* like I actually like cats!

It's my *duty* to make my clients' clients believe my clients. If my clients' clients don't believe me, my clients' clients won't believe my clients. Did you get that? It's my job to read about kitty litter so *compellingly* that these people who hear or see this commercial are going to say, "Wow, I want that kitty litter *now!* I really want that cat food for my cat…it's obviously the best!" I've read it so compellingly as if I really do give a *bleep* about cats. That is my job: to bring a script to life, even if I don't really care about the subject matter. That's my job: to bring those words to life, and make it believable.

Your first expense in voiceovers is getting coaching in order to help you be believable, and read but sound like you're *not* reading. Don't spend all this great inordinate amount of money on hardware, software, resources, memberships, conferences, workshops, plugins, etc. It should be *coaching* from the start. And then if your *coach* determines that you are viable, that you're marketable, that you have skill and talent that is ready to go, *then* you start hitting the pavement.

Along the vein of refinement, there are plenty of technique coaches out there that can teach you plenty. Marc Cashman is somebody who has written a fantastic book called *V-Oh!* It's a wonderful book on voiceovers! It doesn't just cover business aspects such as marketing and networking, and agents etc. He talks extensively about technique, and specific techniques that you can employ to become a better voice talent. I would highly recommend Marc Cashman. I'd highly recommend Julie Williams of the VO Insider[62] for the same reason. She's a great technique coach. Everett Oliver and Dave Fennoy are fantastic technique coaches and directors. Elaine Clark wrote "There's Money Where Your Mouth Is." This is an excellent book that deals with technique.

Ultimately, you want to constantly learn. You're never done learning! Remember what Ray Kroc said. There are plenty of things that you can learn; plenty of new practices, new techniques, and new approaches you can adopt in order to stay fresh.

I'm still learning things. Just the other day, I saw someone post on Instagram that in order to pace herself in E-Learning, she does a figure-eight motion with her hand as she's reading, and this metronomic motion helps her keep a rhythmic pace in order to not go too fast. I didn't know that beforehand! I wasn't familiar with that technique. In seeing this, I was educated and enlightened.

You find little nuggets of truth all the time.

Don't just cruise through your day and churn out auditions. Stop and learn and soak up and sponge what people – your colleagues and your mentors and teachers – are putting out there. Keep on learning. Your career depends on it.

It's so important to network and continue to grow and refine yourself as a voice talent. It is an art. It is the greatest career you will ever have. And I mean that with all my heart.

CHAPTER 6:
2P OR NOT 2P:
THAT IS THE QUESTION

CONTROVERSY! FIRE AND BRIMSTONE! TAR & FEATHER HIM!

Disclaimer: I already know this is going to be a long and most certainly controversial chapter for those who have been involved in the voiceover industry. Breathe easy.

I'll say some things you'll like; I'll say something that will make you want to throw a microphone at me. (Please throw 416s or Neumanns only, as I can catch them, and then turn around and sell them to pay for my hospital stay. Thanks!) Either way, please know that I am not endorsing any one approach; I'm simply talking about what has worked for me as a voiceover businessman.

I'm fully cognizant that I'm putting myself out there on the chopping block, and going out on a limb. So be it. Here goes…

THE REST WAS HISTORY

Voiceovers. It's not what it used to be. Is it worse, or is it better?

In this chapter, I'm going to talk about the P2Ps, or Pay-To-Play" Voiceover Marketplaces. If you're not familiar with them, you're going to be. For many, they are an *essential* part of their voiceover success. For others, they are a disgrace. For all, they aren't going anywhere anytime soon.

As J. Michael Collins stated in a recent webinar with Jon Florian on VoiceoverXtra[63], lower rates and fighting harder for good pay is "the new normal." The question here is what will you and I do to adapt and overcome? The market has changed.

We do have rate guides, but with the proliferation of naïve voice talent and aspiring businessowners not committed to towing the rates line, pay has become somewhat of a moving goalpost. So, it truly is up to us to fight to get them fixed again in the consciences of our customers.

Many years ago, when puppies were the oldest animals, you'd get a call from your agent, hop in the car, drive to a recording studio, record in front of producers and technicians and end clients (maybe), and then return home and pray and wait.

Then, when you're awarded the job, you hop in the car, drive to a recording studio, record in front of producers and technicians and end clients (maybe), and then return home and pray and wait…for a paycheck.

Now, with the advent of the Internet, home studios are springing up all over the globe, in closets and custom builds alike. They can run anywhere from a clothes closet to a pipe-and-drape setup to a WhisperRoom or StudioBricks studio. And they truly allow flexibility in recording and auditioning.

It used to be a situation where you could cock your eyebrow, give your head a little George-Clooney-shake swagger, and say "Call my agent." Now, the question looms on the horizon, especially in the state of Washington as it pertains to the National Right-to-Work foundation, are agents even necessary?

As VO Agent Alliance states:

According to the National Right-To-Work Legal Defense Foundation (nrtw.org), "a Right-to-Work law secures the right of employees to decide for themselves whether or not to join or financially support a union." Each state has its own statutes regarding this issue and should be researched online or at your library or through contacting SAG-AFTRA directly. Right-to-Work states include: Alabama, Arizona, Arkansas, Florida, Georgia, Idaho, Iowa, Kansas, Louisiana, Mississippi, Nebraska, Nevada, North Carolina, North Dakota, Oklahoma, South Carolina, South Dakota, Tennessee, Texas, Utah, Virginia, and Wyoming. The remaining states are considered "closed shops." Nearly half the country falls under Right-to-Work, which more or less renders the unions, in our case SAG-AFTRA, somewhat useless.[64]

So where does that leave us, represented and non-represented alike?

TIME TO BEAT THE STREETS

What does all of this mean for the hardworking agent-dependent voiceover artist? Ultimately, it means that they need to look for more work on their own.

Voiceover agents used to be the gateway to voiceover work. "You want voiceover work? Gotta get an agent." *Lo contrario* anymore: if you want work, you're going to have to find it yourself. The name of the game now is: *develop a love for marketing.* Agents are no longer the "end all be all" that they used to be. The truth of the matter is that A) there are a *lot* of shady, crappy agents out there (none of mine are!) and B) you can make and find a lot of work yourself, through direct marketing.

Marketing is something that's always been natural for me. I'm a campaigner, and I love seeing a good thing prosper. Sure, sometimes I get butterflies in my stomach just during and after I send that "submit" button on my Zoho campaign, I hope to see positive results, and don't want to make people unsubscribe. But I have bellies to fill, mouths to feed, and bills to pay. And reaching out to prospective clients is all part of the job, and all in a day's work.

Self-imposed and self-motivated marketing really enables me to connect with people I otherwise might never have. It's truly rewarding to receive a "Sure, send me your demo reel" back over email. It's even more rewarding to receive an audition notice or a casting offer on the coattails of any marketing campaigns I send out.

I *love* marketing. I truly do. There's nothing more satisfying than turning over a rock and finding a bunch of gleeful new clients waving at me, splitting at the ears from a giant grin. (That's how it always happens, right?) But marketing isn't the end-all-be-all either. It is actually 80-90% of what I do every day, yes: always on the hunt, looking for the next client to pounce (gently) on. But it isn't the easiest thing to do, and not everyone feels confident enough in it.

For that, there's a middle ground between direct marketing and agents: the P2Ps.

HUH? P2P? IS THAT A NEW RAP ARTIST?

Ya down with P2P? Yeah, you know me.

Let's do a bit of defining, for those joining us late. I've mentioned this previously in the book and you may have said, like The Grinch, "Uh…holiday whobee whatee?"

P2Ps, aka "Pay-to-play's", are websites that represent online voiceover marketplaces that came about around 2010. These are sites devoted to facilitating business between the voice talent, and the client, who in this case we'll call the voice seeker.

The most notable P2Ps are listed below, and you can visit them by adding a .com after each one:

- Voice123
- Voices (herein known as VDC to mitigate some of the coming "sting")
- Bodalgo
- VOPlanet
- Voiceovers
- ACX

I add ACX into this mix because they are something of a P2P, but ultimately you pay nothing to join; you must have a Tax ID number at the very least. They are nevertheless essentially an online voiceover marketplace. There are more, and there *will* be even more, but I'll mention them later, and not so kindly.

A voice seeker will join one of these P2Ps, and they will post a casting notice. They may actually post it on multiple P2Ps hoping to cast a wider net. They'll ultimately choose only one voice from wherever they cast their net. The voiceover marketplace usually exacts a percentage in the neighborhood of 20%, and in some cases a managed job fee (I'll get to that later), and assesses that on top of the project budget.

> *There's a middle ground between direct marketing and agents: the P2Ps.*

The voice talent who has a paid membership on any of these P2Ps is allowed to receive audition notices numbering anywhere from a few a day to a few dozen a day, depending on their profile specifications and the parameters they set up governing how many audition notices they actually want to receive. They audition, and if they are chosen by the voice seeker to fulfill that role, an agreement is setup through the P2P's interface – or independent of it, as is the case of a few of them – and the work begins. Once the work is finished, on some P2P sites, the voice seeker releases payment

Running a Successful Voiceover Business   Joshua Alexander

once files are received, and both the voice seeker and the voice talent are done.

On sites that facilitate independent communication, agreements and contracts between voice seeker and voice talent (for example Voice123, VOPlanet and Bodalgo, and ACX to some extent), a direct invoice can be sent from the voice talent to the voice seeker. The voice talent is paid, and the job is done.

Now, here's where it gets tricky, and every voice talent who's been around longer than 3 years, especially in 2017, will start to feel the salt in their wounds.

For that, I apologize.

Here goes.

ALONG CAME A SPIDER

If you've never heard the story, let us gather our sustenance and drinks, quell the mirth, and sit by the fire...and I shall regale you with a tale of old.

There used to be an organization called *VoiceBank*. They started in 1998 and were pretty much the leader in terms of online connection points for voiceover artists and voice casting agents, both for startup talent as well as famous actors. They had lots of contributors and community members spanning video production companies, ad agencies, etc. In August of 2017 VDC bought the rights to VoiceBank, and that's where things went south for many folks. Tom Dheere also has an excellent article on this[65], as does J. Michael Collins[66]. It truly frightened Miss Muffett away...and a lot of her cohorts as well.

VoiceBank was an online connection point, a *community* really, facilitating voice talent to connect with agents, to receive reviews of their work, critiques of their demos, connecting them to agents, demo producers, etc. It really was a great community. But in the ensuing year, as VDC started presenting audition opportunities to talent, something smelled funny. They were called on the carpet, and, in fact, exposed for skimming profits, as well as for exorbitant "managed job fees". What I mean by that is that they would post a national TV commercial that would rightfully charge a video production company, say, $5000 for the voiceover, and then post the job on VDC for $300. Their hope was undoubtedly that a newbie would see that and say, "Wow, $300?!?! That's awesome!"

What the newbie didn't know, to their peril, and to the collective frustration of the entire established voiceover community, was that that TV commercial *should* be paying them $5000. Information truly is power. Todd Schick wrote an excellent blog on this, exposing the whole fraud[67]. Additionally, according to their own site, "the Project Management Fee starts at $300, and increases with project complexity."

It's now 2021, and VDC is still arguably the top player in the online voiceover marketplace. But in the words of our favorite green Jedi puppet, "No...there is another." Other P2Ps have sprung up to unseat them, others have been around and would like nothing more than to see them die a fiery death. Their CEO, David Ciccarelli, remains elusive and won't comment or show any support for the voiceover community. They recently partnered with an agency called VocalID[68], and some speculation existed that this partnership was in an effort to harvest all the voice samples submitted through their portal, to generate synthetic voices: a truly creepy and nefarious notion, and not outside of the realm of possibilities. However, they are no longer working with Voices.com for ethical reasons, and they are actually good people.

However, all that being said, my job in this is not to write a chapter or to rehash an all-too-familiar scandal. My goal in this chapter is to present *vision* and to promote possibilities.

What if, in the voiceover community, we took a step back, took a deep breath, and fully realized that VDC, like anything on the internet, and - *yea verily* - like the Internet itself, was a tool to be used wisely? It's not going away. So, what if instead of attacking those who are a part of it – we affirmed and built up, and encouraged? There is *still* a fair amount of vitriol directed at those still active on VDC, and such vitriol often recirculates, like sludge, amongst the various Facebook voiceover groups. Oil must keep rising to the top, I guess. Some comments are even cutthroat. The level of animosity directed from some veterans at some newbies is appalling and disappointing. On top of that, some agents won't even consider you if you're active on VDC. I just don't share the same vitriol. The only vitriol I feel is towards sites like Fiverr, JustSaySpots, The Voice Realm, Cheapvoiceovers, etc.

The P2Ps – including VDC – are not going away. Some see them as the perfect opportunity to make a living doing voiceovers. Others see them as the bane of the entire industry. What I see, is *opportunity.* Opportunity to, once a job is finalized for a client, convert said client to a *direct* client that I take *off* of said P2P. I have been able to do this many, many, times, and I've made many, many thousands of dollars from several repeat jobs from clients who initially booked me through, mainly, VDC. I use this P2P as a funnel. As a *tool* for direct client harvesting. Adapt and overcome.

Let's set two things straight. There are more than a few other sites on the web today that facilitate voiceover work, and I strongly dissuade anyone from using them. They include Fiverr, The Voice Realm, VoiceBunny, VoiceJungle, UpWork, SpeedySpots, JustSaySpots, Freelancer, JustSaySpots, and the like. Especially The Voice Realm. Cheapvoiceovers.com are a subset of The Voice Realm, but as they have other such trashy sites, I won't mention all of them, I'll just mention the main bad boy here. Boy they're a nasty, juvenile, disorganized bunch. They're in the UK, and perhaps something is lost in translation by the time it makes its way through the Interwebs to me, but *yeeshk*. Dropped them like a hot potato after too long. Among other things, they yell at you with ALL-CAPS emails, their rates are abysmal in most cases, their clients are uber-demanding and nigh unpleasant in some cases. They never pay on time and this necessitates manual follow-up, and once a project is over, you're forbidden from even thanking your client and engaging in "keep in touch" communication lest Voice Realm watch you two take your business elsewhere and they lose out. They're pathetically paranoid and irretrievably childish.

And JustSaySpots and Fiverr (again, the F-word in the voiceover industry) are atrocious. They are responsible for the largest erosion of the industry pay scale. Sites like these, that are demeaning to the voiceover talents they represent, and that promote bargain-basement pricing, are to be avoided at all costs.

So, the question then is: with all the scandal that VDC has been involved in, why continue with them? Why feed the beast? Why be part of something that is so apparently harmful to the voiceover industry? Why sleep with the enemy? Where I personally failed was in providing VDC a video interview in 2018 that they still use for promotional purposes. I wish my eyes were a bit more open then, and, obviously, time changes opinions. I'm no exception. I will continue to use them and audition and produce through them, but I don't feel the same about them that I did when I first began. I'm grateful for the opportunities that come my way through them, but, ultimately, I can't in good conscience endorse them, knowing what I know now.

One word, and I'll repeat it again: *tool*. Again, VDC is a tool. Any tool, on or off the Internet, and just like the Internet itself, needs to be used wisely. I can use a tool and not thereby endorse it. I can use a hammer to pound a nail in the wall. I may miss the nail and bludgeon my thumb. I hate that hammer for a while, and I'll have a lasting resentment of it, but I'll probably still use it, because it gets the job done for me. That doesn't mean I will slap an "I-heart-hammers" bumper sticker on my car.

But let me make myself very clear again, for the sake of having it in print. However scandalous their reputation may be, I still use them. But this is *not* an endorsement of VDC or any other P2P. I've seen lowball rates across virtually all of the P2Ps, and while the majority of jobs I see pay at or near the industry pay scale, there are still a few atrocious ones that make you scoff. I think one of VDC's only saving graces (albeit a seesaw of enabling underbidding and overbidding, and Voice123 is in the same boat) is that it allows you to state your own price for a project, in line with rates found at the GVAA Rate Guide[69], Gravy for The Brain's rate guide[70], and Voiceovers.com's DeCypherVO Rate Calculator.[71] These rate guides are critical, and instrumental, in helping me, and you, to figure out what you should be making on any given project for which you're provided broadcast specs and usage details. One of the main pluses for VOPlanet is that, in its auditioning process, you're not *allowed* to bid lower than the stated budget; but you are allowed to bid higher: a defining attribute of an organization insistent on fair wages for voice talent.

If it says it's an Explainer Video, and the budget is $100 to $250, you should be bidding $300, since that's around what Explainer Videos pay. A good producer on the casting end of that job listing will recognize that you're experienced and bidding according to what you should be paid, and they'll cast you. They may see desperation, novice level, and lack of team player qualities in one who underbids. Or they may not. Is it a crapshoot? Sometimes. Is there balance? Yes. Allow me to explain further.

Paul Strikwerda says, "People who only compete on price...are making a huge mistake. By doing so, they are devaluing what they have to offer, even before the client has had a chance to respond. As soon as you start competing on price, you treat your valuable service or product as a dime-a-dozen commodity."[72] He goes on later to say "Do you want your service to be known for being the cheapest on the market, or for high quality? Competing on price is a losing battle."[73]

There exists a choice that we have to make when facing the prospect of impending unemployment and starvation. I've made a choice to diversify and provide for my family. Pursuant to that choice, you can stand over there and be mad on principle, and I'll be over here making money. Sound good? You can use VDC, as I do, as a *tool* – and just bid according to the rate guides we've been provided, in order to secure for yourself the rate(s) you deserve for the project(s) you are awarded. Granted, this will require you to bid higher than some projects' budgets in order to be paid your fair wage. Consequently, you may lose out on said project, which I'm sure has happened to me hundreds of times. I am in this to make money and to be a financial success. I've also seen the scales balanced nicely. In some projects, I've made concessions and been paid a bit under. And some projects I've been paid quite a bit over what the rate guides say I should make. Balance. I would also rather be tilling fresh soil there, taking jobs for fair wages, rather than some clucking spring chicken pecking my job out from underneath me with a $100 bid.

Whether you like the P2Ps or not, they are also all run by businessmen who want to make a profit too. It's capitalism, pure and simple. It is deeply, deeply unfortunate that in the name of capitalism - nay, *greed* - the management of some of VDC's projects, direct on down from the CEO, have proven in the past to be shady and downright unethical.

But we don't have to let the politics of the online voiceover marketplace phenomenon jade us. Yes, there are politics at play, just like there are anywhere else. But we can govern our emotions and figure out what approach is best for ourselves, not condemning someone else for an approach that works best for them (it's this last part that I'll cover last).

But first, back to quoting.

QUOTING WITH INTEGRITY

Lest VDC dominates this entire chapter, suffice it to say that across all spectrums, in every place, whether it's Voices, Voiceovers, Voice Realm, Voice123, Bodalgo, VOPlanet, ACX, Upwork, Freelancer, Fiverr, VoiceJungle, SpeedySpots, CastingCallClub, JustSaySpots, Craigslist, VOQuent, and the dreaded VoiceBunny with their ever-fluctuating quality-assurance standards, you'll find a sliding scale of posted rates. Where clients sometimes get their budget numbers of what they assume a voiceover should cost is beyond me.

Let the rate guides proposed earlier be your guide. Once again, the P2Ps aren't going anywhere. They've proven themselves to be an effective link between talent and seekers. How you handle them as a voice talent businessperson is going to determine your success or failure in the voiceover industry. You can keep in step with those who will help you navigate the estimating field, with solid rates. Talk is *not* cheap. Don't help it get there by selling yourself out and undercutting your brothers and sisters in voiceovers by diving towards the bargain basement just to get the job first. Trust the pro who said, "if you're giving 500 dollars-worth of services away for free, you're not only creating expectations, you're in fact saying: this is what I think my work is worth. Meanwhile, you're robbing a colleague of the chance to make five hundred bucks."[74] While Paul Strikwerda is talking about *donation* of services here, the principle is the same. Don't sell your soul. Don't set a precedent with buyers that you have lower value than you do, and that they can nickle-and-dime you to death. Elaine Clark expresses it very well along the same wavelength: "Giving away our services or selling them below market value in order to get the job is shortsighted and hurts everyone."[75]

Online marketplace organizations such as VOPlanet, Bodalgo, and now CastVoices - the brainchild of longtime agent and tech entrepreneur Liz Atherton - are determined to fight for fair wages. They are committed to ensuring that voice talent receive the pay that they should, and are not scammed. They've seen the upheaval caused by the acquisition of VoiceBank, and the proliferation of home studios brought about by the internet revolution.

They're determined to be a catalyst for preservation of fair voiceover pay, and they are ethical, honest game changers who desire equity. They join voice casting agencies like *In Both Ears* who genuinely fight for fair voiceover rates. For that, God bless them. I hate it as much as you do when a client expects to pay X when they should be paying Y. I much prefer Y. It's a much nicer letter.

A STEADY STREAM

How you handle these P2Ps – any of them – is up to you. But ultimately, they are all trying to do the same thing: connect voice seekers with voice talent.

I have made so much money through the P2Ps. As a voiceover businessman, I cannot discount their importance to me. Some have ended poorly, but needed to end. For example, I fired The Voice Realm even after having made over $14,000 from them, because I couldn't tolerate their juvenile behavior, their smutty advertising, and their disorganization and condescension. In fact, I even recently discovered a Google ad with *my name associated with it*, pointing to them, even after I had left them:

Joshua Alexander Voiceover | Easy Online Voice Casting
[Ad] www.thevoicerealm.com/ ▾
Get Free Auditions & Instant Access to Professional **Voice Over** Talent Offering Best Rates.
Better Rates. Free Auditions. Only The Best Voice Talent. Know More. Fast Voice Casting.
Translation Services. 24/7 Support. World's Best Talent. Best Agency Rates. Male Voices.
Male Voice Over Talent · Never Hired a Voice? · Search Massive Database · Male Voice Over

Cheeky, Voice Realm. Cheeky. Bad show. They are underhanded and unethical, piggybacking on my SEO and search terms, like aa remora to a shark. (I threatened to bite them legally: they complied and removed their ad.)

But overall, using each one of these P2Ps has been a massive benefit to my bottom line, and, for at least VDC, the fact that I can convert clients to direct clients afterwards has been of immeasurable value. Had some of my repeat clients never found me through VDC to begin with, I would not have made so many multiple thousands of dollars by providing them service *subsequent* to, and *independent of*, VDC.

Also - if you work the system, and if you audition frequently and treat each audition as a paid job, the memberships totally pay for themselves. It is astonishing to me to think that I initially balked at VDC's $399 annual membership fee. You can pay that off with a single job, and then some. My income from VDC alone is closing in on one hundred thousand dollars in nearly four years' time, and all I've paid in membership fees is $1596. A sound investment.

The P2Ps provide lots of audition opportunities for us non-union folk, due to the ease of project posting for the client. However, I do understand that for some voice talent, auditioning so much can seem like drudgery. I tend to look at it differently and put a positive spin on it. I take the total amount I've made in voiceovers, and divide it by the total amount of auditions I've done. Doing so averages out to about $18 per audition. I perceive it literally like I'm being paid $18 each time I step into that studio to perform an audition. Would you try out for a role if they were paying you $18? I also go into every audition saying to myself "I've already been awarded these jobs." It's a willful intention; not a blind hope; it's also not a cocky overconfidence. It's simply *belief.*

I can really truly appreciate what many entrepreneurs have said, and that's "don't put all your eggs into one basket." I don't rely solely on the P2Ps; I rely on direct marketing, repeat business, searching, networking, conversations, and more. The more diverse you can make your income streams, the more adaptable you'll be, and the longer you'll remain in business. I am certainly not an expert in this; there are people like Collins who truly pay attention to their numbers and are not a voiceover *businessman*, but rather a *CEO*.

GOT VITRIOL? STOW IT.

Lastly: don't eviscerate someone for using a different voiceover business model than you. We rise and fall on our own merits. If you see someone continuing to rise, applaud them: they're obviously killing it! If you can't summon the nerve, are you suspicious of them for sidestepping your system, or some other perceived standard for business success? Or is it jealousy? Are we really a community? Or do we just say we are but we're really a bunch of backstabbing gossips? There are more veterans and seasoned professionals on VDC alone than everyone might think. I have been told that there are even industry veterans on Fiverr under pseudonyms, for obvious reasons. Do I hunt them down to expose them? No. I don't care enough to. A witch hunt is not my calling nor desire; I'm busy with marketing and voicing.

The sheepish mention of being on VDC for fear of verbal abuse needs to end, and here's why: when I first joined a local voiceover meetup, I was eviscerated within a half hour of arriving, by the leader and others, for mentioning that I was on VDC. To receive such a salient greeting and to know that that subject was hovering in the air for the duration of my very first Meetup there, left me with a sour mouth and an upset tummy. I tried to return to their group a few times, but just felt uncomfortable at the very notion. Consequently, I started my own Meetup with the goal of being more affirming, and I formed the Global Voiceover Artists Network[76] on Facebook with the same intent.

What happened to me in that Meetup is not an isolated incident. I have seen boiling froth spewed at countless voice talent on and offline who have mentioned that they were part of this site or that site. The mob mentality is alive and well, and there's an "old guard" out in force today that adamantly insists that you do it their way or you're "out." I fully expect blowback from this chapter yet again. When I see any of this behavior, if I'm connected to such a person online, or if they're in a group I'm involved with, I'll make a practice of distancing myself from them, because I find them toxic. It's *especially* toxic if they're a voiceover veteran, and they're directing their vitriol at a newbie, who needs to be informed, not inundated; affirmed, not attacked; led, not lashed; educated, not eviscerated. I appreciate Tom Dheere's recent blog[77] on this. I've unfriended some people because

> *We can govern our emotions and figure out what approach is best for ourselves, not condemning someone else for an approach that works best for them.*

their natural inclination is to tear down out of their own misgiving, rather than graciously assume the best of people.

Are we a community? Don't all of us have the very same goal of putting bread on our table for us and our loved ones? One of the most mature approaches I've seen is, again, by J Michael Collins, who, even having sued VDC for continuing to promote themselves using an endorsement video that includes him from many years ago (he's since withdrawn his endorsement), he's respectful about it. He's eloquent. He's articulate. He's a diplomatic statesman about it. And with the fallout from Voice123's "upgrades" and CEO Rolf Veldman's somewhat apathy[78] for fair project rates and usage, Collins has been a diplomatic, stately liaison there as well[79]. He treats other voice talent with respect. There are many, unfortunately, who do not: they are far too consumed with just being residually and perpetually resentful – and their tendency is to dump.

Don't call those who are on VDC or Fiverr or what have you, "sleeping with the enemy", sellouts or turncoats. The terms are derogatory and do nothing to redirect and educate. If we want to collectively stem the tide, let's have real, frank discussions with those people who *invite* us to have such conversations with them. In other words, let's wait until they've *asked* for our precious opinion. Don't sit behind your computer and judge me, or others, for being on VDC. This isn't a UK miner strike, and I'm no scab[80]. I want the same things you want: fair pay and ethics and transparency. Don't hurl accusations at another voiceover artist for being on The Voice Realm (I won't, even though the organization sucks). Don't form cliques and talk about others behind their back for being on Fiverr.

Otherwise, you're just barging in on foreign soil and are no better than a crusader. It doesn't make your approach right because you think their approach is wrong. Even Hitler was convinced he was right. There are reasons why they're on there, and neither you nor I know their story. Most likely, that person just simply needs to eat. You can withhold scorn now and educate about higher-priced, more delicious food later. Regardless of your own opinions about a particular P2P, don't harass the person using it. They are trying out tools to their own benefit, to provide for themselves and their family. They are learning. They will learn in time.

Now here comes the hard part. Many of you reading this are priming your harrummph. From the moment I mentioned VDC, you started readying your guns, and now you're locked and loaded. You're sitting back and sighing and clicking your tongue in disapproval, and all kinds of names for me are being bandied about in your brain, for even halfway suggesting that we use P2Ps, especially VDC. Let me ask you: will you label me a serial purveyor of bad advice because of this? Or will you trust that I want fair wages too, that I'm doing the best I can, and that you have hidden colleagues to your left and right on VDC as well who are equally trying to provide for themselves? We're not a cancer. We're just doing our best. We're all just trying to do our best in the ways we can. Could it be that I want the same as you, to convert P2P clients to direct clients? Will you extend me the benefit of the doubt? Let's use some Proverbs 15:1 here:

A gentle answer turns away wrath, but a harsh word stirs up anger.

Time to build each other up and stand together and call ourselves a community. The agents are dwindling but still fighting for us. The P2Ps are providing never before seen avenues to connecting with clients *directly* and in easy-to-use interfaces. There is so much work out there, and we're all trying to ethically snag a piece of the pie for ourselves. We all need to eat. This is not a clarion call for *kumbaya* - but wouldn't it be nice if we could have a great feast at the same great table together, laughing and drinking together like hobbits.

THAT'S MY FINAL ANSWER, REGIS

If there's one site that I have stratospheric hopes for, it's *CastVoices.* Liz Atherton and her team have diligently sought to not only carve out a piece of the market for themselves to build a successful business, they have done it on the premise that they long to bring a sea change to the rates situation for voiceover artists. And they are doing so.

If I was going to throw anyone's name in the ring as the voiceover marketplace that I would endorse, it would be Liz's. I see big things on the horizon for CastVoices, and it's been a pleasant experience thus far watching it grow and start to succeed as a contender in this great busy online marketplace world we call the P2Ps.

There. Are we still friends? Or will I be *persona non grata?*

ducks to avoid flying 416's

For a complete course on successfully auditioning and getting cast through the P2Ps, visit www.supervoiceovertraining.com.

CHAPTER 7:
AUDITIONING, CASTING &
DELIVERING

THE FIVE T'S TO TRIUMPH

There are five T's to triumph in being cast as a voice talent. The first one is *Technique*. The second one is *Technical*. The third one is *Timing*. The fourth is *Tier*. And the fifth is *Trust*.

Technique.

Technique is very critical. You can simply "read" as a voice talent, or you can read and *bring a script to life*. You can read and just *slay* the listener, and absolutely make them *spellbound*.

Here's a suggestion along the lines of technique: have a picture of somebody you care about in your studio. Deliver it to them. You'll be able to deliver it more conversationally and naturally to a person you know and trust. You're reading a script, you're bouncing back and forth between the script and a picture of somebody that you really relate to: that helps you bring a script to life.

Another trick that I've employed that really helps me to deliver a script well, is to pretend like I'm actually in a directed session. Now, directed sessions obviously don't happen until you're formally cast, but you can still pretend that you're in one. What I do is, before I actually go into the script, I'll put my hand over my ear, or over one of my headphones, as if I'm listening to my client. And I'll say, "you guys ready? *[pause]* Okay, here we go!" I'll *pretend* they're there. I'll *pretend* they've answered. And something in me registers that this is actually a live recording. I'm on the spot. It actually encourages me to do far better, to perform under the gun, as it were. That way I deliver a better, livelier, more believable script that way. If I can pretend that I'm in a directed session, I find that helps me out a lot.

The most important thing in any audition that you submit is to be yourself. Oscar Wilde said, *Be yourself; everyone else is already taken*. Don't try to go in and sound like Don LeFontaine or Matthew

McConaughey, or Morgan Freeman, or Catherine Zeta Jones, or Uma Thurman, or David Attenborough, or Sam Elliot; leave those characters behind unless you are *specifically* asked to sound like them. You'll sometimes get those casting notices from agents and through P2Ps that specifically request a soundalike. *That's* when you sound like James Earl Jones.

But there's only one you - it's very, very, very important for you to be *yourself.* The reason for this is because these casting directors are being barraged by auditioners. The more *you* that you can sound, the more unique you will be. Marc Cashman says that we each have our own unique voiceprint. If you can just be yourself and let that "unique you" shine through, then you're not impersonating someone else. That way you stand apart from the herd…and get heard.

Technical.

Technical is equally critical. If your audio quality is full of pops and clicks and s's and bad noise floor, then you're probably not going to get cast. There's a very good chance that you won't get cast, because your audio quality is compromised, even though you may have read especially well. Poor technical quality is a big detractor for a potential casting director, because they're unsure if you'll be able to produce quality audio.

You need a good sterile audio environment with minimal noise floor. You need acoustical treatment. You need to eliminate reflective surfaces from your recording environment. Then, for software, you need plugins such as a de-esser, de-breath, de-plosive, de-hiss, etc. You need broadcast-ready EQ plugins. Your audio needs to sound phenomenal. Put your best foot forward!

BoothJunkie and other YouTube channels and advisors can really help you *perfect* your recording environment. I mention these in my blog article on "How do I get started in Voiceovers?"[81] There are those people who are devoted to helping you build a pristine recording environment. Some of them I've mentioned earlier such as Jordan Reynolds, Tim Tippets, Roy Yokelson, etc. For a nominal fee, they can calibrate your audio environment – and your DAW template - and make it *shine.*

Don't just learn to bring a script to life. Bring your *recording environment* to life. Make sure that everything in there is as antiseptic as possible, as stripped of noise as possible, as *perfect* as possible. That way you'll get cast.

Timing.

The third key is *Timing*. There's no way around it. There are a *lot* of people that are submitting for any of these casting notices through agents, through P2Ps, through repeat clients, etc. If you have technique and technical in place, great: you've got a "voice up" on the competition. Believe it or not, there are actually people out there submitting auditions from their smartphone. *Wow.* Their quality clearly isn't there. But even so: they may be sending in their audition immediately upon receiving the casting notice. If you're not sending in auditions until you get home from work, or you're sending them the next day, or a few days late, in some cases, even a few hours later, you're way down in the running.

The earlier that you can submit, the less likely you are going to fall into the trap of "audition fatigue." As these casting directors are receiving a massive amount of casting auditions from voiceover talent out there, and as they're all sounding relatively the same, it behooves you to get it in as soon as possible before this exponential curve of willingness to listen to more auditioners takes a nosedive. It is of *tremendous* importance for you to submit as soon as you possibly can.

When I was awarded a national TV commercial for Nutrisystem in 2017, there were 104 auditioners for that role. I was number seven. I remember that because there were six before me, so I'm sure that helped me. Had I been 104, I don't know that I would have been cast. I don't know. I may never know. Maybe they'll listen to all 104! Maybe they're really only willing to listen to 50. But you don't want to be *after* the point at which they say "I can't take it anymore, okay? *Just pick one already.*"

By the way: that particular Nutrisystem client? I booked them off of Voices.com. I took them *off* of VDC, and have since booked $28,367 in direct jobs with them. It does work.

Remember, if you have technique, but not technical, you won't get cast. If you have technical but not technique, you won't get cast. If you have both, but you send it in way too late, you won't get cast. Keep that in mind!

Tier.

The fourth "T" is *Tier*. What tier are you on? I alluded to this earlier with Voice123. I am on the $2200/year tier; I wasn't always – I used to be on the $395/year tier, and then I upgraded to $888. I saw remarkable success after upgrading to the $888 level. So, I kept upgrading. It really depends on what tier you are, and what investment you're prepared to make in this particular P2P. Voices.com, Voice123.com, and Voiceovers.com have tiered membership levels. The people on the top tier are those who pay the most, sometimes around $5000 for a "platinum" membership. They get first dibs on the voiceover casting notices that come through, because they're paying top dollar. It's like being in "first class" in the casting plane. They paid for that, so they get everything first. Then it filters down to the next tier, and then next, and the next, until it finally hits the "free" members who haven't paid for a membership. Your likelihood of getting cast for a role through a tier-system P2P decreases depending on which tier you're on.

Hold on a second, though. Let's not put the cart before the horse. Don't go spending a whole bunch of money. If you haven't had coaching, don't go upgrading to the highest platinum tier just yet. If you don't have a commercial demo, or if you haven't gotten jobs under your belt already and don't have any kind of pattern developed of booking jobs yet, just wait. These tiers demand something of you. If you're not prepared to audition a lot, that will hurt your chances. You have to be willing to audition. And you have to be willing to audition *soon* (Timing). So, don't jump to these higher tiers unless it is really time to do so.

Trust.

The fifth "T" is *Trust*. Will your client be able to trust you? As you're auditioning for a script, every script is accompanied by directions, by casting specs, etc. If they are requesting a woman in her 20s to 30s, and she's British, but she sounds a little childish, with a little bit of rasp to her voice, well, there you go. It might be a Caribbean male, who's 60, who is a little bit kind of gruff, slurs his speech and is a bit short under the collar. And then they might want you to deliver it sort of melancholy. Or aggressive. They may call for laid back, or sleepy. Whatever!

These people put those casting specs and directions in there for a reason. The fifth "T", *Trust* has to deal with your client being able to trust that you are reading what they say: are you delivering as they're requesting? Are you following directions? Can you follow directions?

Don't make a client say "What????" when they review your audition. That's not going to help you. You don't want to be remembered as being hard to direct. Obey, comply, read their casting specs, and read their directions that they've taken the time to include. Every time a casting notice is born, every time a voiceover need is born, the casting director or the producer or whoever it is, already has in their mind what they want it to sound like. So, if you go in guns-a-blazing with a Matthew McConaughey voice when they clearly stated they were really wanting James Earl Jones, you're completely off the mark. In doing that, you are wasting your time and theirs.

With every audition, go in *intending*. I'm very fond of saying *intention trumps hope every time*. Go in *intending* to be awarded a job. Don't go in with hope that you *might* be maybe possibly awarded a job today, if your luck holds. Go into that studio in *full assurance* that this job is yours.

I understand *Imposter Syndrome* is a big thing. I get it. But as long as you condition yourself and train yourself to believe that you have what it takes to read these scripts, *before* you set foot in your studio, you're going to have better odds against all of those people that are just going in on the on the whim of a hope. Not so for you. Go in *intending* to be awarded these jobs.

I have a sign on my studio door that says "I've already been awarded all these projects." That doesn't come from hubris. It doesn't come from arrogance, or cockiness. It's simply confidence. And as Jack Palance used to say in the old commercial for Skin Bracer, "Confidence is very sexy, don't you think?"

It's very sexy to have confidence; they can hear that coming through the tone of your voice. When you deliver your script, they can hear that confidence being projected, and they can hear that you *know* you have what it takes. So, don't *hope* you have what it takes. *Know* that you have what it takes. Morpheus said that to Neo in their sparring scene in *The Matrix:* "Don't think you are; *know* you are."

Most importantly, above all else, give your *all* during every audition. I mentioned earlier, you can't get a 100% job on a 50% audition. You can't give halfway and save your "all" for when they award you the job. They want to hear your all right away. I think Bill Lloyd's coach is the one who said something like "every audition is the awarded job. Being cast for that audition is icing on the cake. That's just a bonus." Every audition *is* the awarded job. Give 100% to every audition that you do, and you have a better chance of being cast.

Provide multiple reads per audition, depending on the length of the script and your desire to provide multiple reads. If your agent is specifically instructing you to do multiple reads, you better do multiple reads. For P2Ps, it's somewhat the same. If your script is fairly short, and you feel like doing multiple reads, I would do it and give them some variety. Do one that complies with their directions, and then do one that is maybe your own interpretation; that way, that gives them more variety, and also shows improvisational ability on your part. I've been awarded jobs where I did exactly as they requested of me in terms of direction. And then I did *another* read of my own creative flavor - and they awarded me based on Read 2, because it was *better* than what they had envisioned! You never know what creativity will afford you when you decide to go out on a limb and give them extra.

"The lead line". Get familiar with this concept. Michael Bell says the following: "One thing I've learned is that your VO audition must capture the casting director's attention in the first 10 seconds, or they will not listen to the rest. They simply don't have time."[82] Your first 10 seconds are critical! You never get a second chance to make a first impression. Your first 10 seconds need to stand out and grab them. It's very important! The first 10 seconds of every audition are so important to make that impression.

Also, extremely important to find in each script is "the money line" as Bill DeWees calls it.[83] This is what everything boils down to. This is the central message in the script. Don't dissect your script *ad nauseum*. Look at it, get the gist of it, get into character, read it, even if it's E-Learning or it's just an explainer video or commercial - get into that character and understand what this script is really about. The *money line* is what the script is really all about. You have to identify that money line before you go in.

Another tip: Unless your agent says specifically *not* to slate your audition, if you're reading two different reads, make sure and begin your first recording with something like "Read #1", and then your second one with "Read #2." Unless they hear that "Read #1" at the beginning of your audition, they won't know there's a Read #2. You may get cast for Read 2! It's important to state how many you have.

Or you could say something like "Joshua Alexander, multiple reads." Let them know that there are a few options coming their way. You don't know which one they're going to choose you for. Make sure they know they have options.

Another tip: don't do every single audition that comes your way. You'll burn out. If you are 47 and part-Latino with a strong accent, don't audition for that 6-year-old Caribbean girl. It's not who you are. They're looking for a 6-year-old Caribbean girl! Don't impersonate somebody that you have no believability in pulling off. Don't do an audition if it's not in your wheelhouse, such as a British accent. If they say only *genuine* British accents, only *authentic* British accents, you better believe they're serious; you better believe that's exactly what they want. Many times they'll put that in caps: "AUTHENTIC

British accents only!" They wouldn't say that if they didn't mean it. If you can pull off a very believable British accent, great! More power to you in life. But that's not what they're asking for. They're not asking for "believable" in all caps. They're asking for AUTHENTIC in all caps. If you're not authentic, then move on to the next one.

You must believe every script that you read. I mentioned before about cats. If you're reading about kitty litter, you are your clients' storyteller! You are their brand ambassador! This clients' clients better believe that you are in *love* with cats, and that you *love* this kitty litter. *It's the best stuff since Moses came down Mount Sinai with the commandments!*

It's of paramount importance to deliver a script with such conviction, otherwise your clients aren't going to cast you - and they'll never be your clients because they don't feel like you believe in their product. Belief is *everything* in reading a script.

Yuri Lowenthal and Tara Platt, in their book *Voice Over Voice Actor, suggest* including a "button" to make them remember you. "Sometimes all it takes is a button on the end of your audition – an extra comment, a punch line, a laugh, or a chuckle – to get your read moved to the top of the list."[84] They may not exactly remember your name. (Hopefully they will, because my advice is *always* put your name in the audition file!) Give them that little added bonus, again, that sets you apart and makes you unique: that little button, as it were, will get you higher in the running, because you're just that much more unique.

Also - *protect* your auditions when you need to. This is super important in the voiceover world, and especially with the P2Ps. Fade them out at the end if you feel you need to, if perhaps the client is a little bit suspect, or if they're stating that only *full* reads will be considered. And maybe this is a first-time user of one of these P2Ps, with no reviews to their name. Be careful. I wouldn't necessarily watermark your auditions: that takes time and is a bit annoying for a prospective casting director. But you can fade them out at the end, or you can swap contact info, which is even better. You can say call us at "phone number", you can say "Company name cares about you," etc. You can say "Visit us at website." That way you're protecting your interests before they cast you so that they *can* cast you, so that they *will* cast you, so that they won't run away with it and use your recordings without paying you. Not everyone is like that though. Nine times out of 10 you're going to deal with an ethical buyer on the pay-to-plays. But you have to universally protect yourself against the few that will spoil it for everybody.

I come across this next issue a lot when I talk to people who are having issues in being cast. Don't spin your wheels. Don't spend an incredible and endless amount of time recording or editing each audition to death. Don't dissect your script until it's blue in the face. Give yourself a little bit of credit that you know what you're doing and that you can bring a script to life. You may be naturally inclined to read a script five to ten times before sending that audition. But here's an idea: try it *once* a few times! Get yourself into the habit of deconditioning yourself from previous *modus operandi*, and deliver your script maybe one time through for an audition - and see if you nail it! Then you'll be able to do an audition and nail it on the first take after a while.

I often do only one take for my auditions. I usually feel I've nailed it. I've read their directions and their casting specs. Make sure that you're not just spinning your wheels and killing yourself in the process by over-analyzing and spending way too much time. Remember the third T in the five T's of triumph. *Timing.* There are a *lot* of people getting in line in front of you while you're hesitating. *Carpe dium.* Don't waste time! It behooves you to get that audition promptly to the decision maker.

Remember, every audition is a marketing opportunity. Marketing might not be your thing. Cold emails, and social media marketing and all that stuff might not be your thing. *But every single blessed audition is a marketing opportunity in and of itself.* Every audition is you putting yourself out there in front of potential clients with every single one. As I mentioned earlier, there are several possible outcomes, but it's all still marketing. Every audition is a marketing opportunity: every single one.

So, if you feel like you're burnt out on auditions, and you don't really have the gumption to give some more, try to think of them in the context of marketing, because every audition gets you in front of someone who could change your life with lots of work. There is no single greater tangible example of what you can do, than an audition.

Also important is bidding ethically. Don't be that guy that's underbidding other voice talent. You see all kinds of jobs on Voices.com that are $100-$249. Often times those are grossly underpaying anyway: read my chapter entitled "2P or not 2P: That is the Question", and see what I and many others have to say about Voices.com's approach. Don't bid $100 just so you get the job. Don't ever think that your inexperience or your short tenure in the voiceover industry demands that you undercharge what you're worth. Don't *ever* think that. It's *so* important to uphold these market rates that we all deserve; to fight for what we should be paid.

The service costs what the service costs, and your tenure in the service doesn't raise or lower your value or deserved rates. What determines the rate is the value assigned to it by the market. So again, please don't be that guy who's underbidding just to get jobs. It's desperation, and it's tacky. Producers can see that under-bidding and say, "this guy isn't a team player, he's a cheapo. I want somebody who's going to be good. This guy doesn't sound like he knows what he's worth."

You'd be surprised: I've actually been awarded jobs where I've bid *above* the recommended bidding range. I daresay it's because the client on the other end saw that I knew what I was worth. She's accustomed to paying that on other sites, or directly to clients for this or that type of video. She sees that I know how much I'm worth! That's a good sign for a potential client to see.

The bottom line on all of this is that you must get familiar with the rate guides that are out there. Know the GVAA Rate Guide, the Gravy For The Brain Rate Guide, etc. Those are very, *very* important to get very familiar with, so that you're not spit-balling or shooting in the dark, saying "Oh boy, uh, I don't know, maybe I'll have 100 bucks, whaddaya think, is that OK?" *Know your worth*. For every client, you are going to be their herald, their ambassador, their spokesman, their storyteller, etc. Your voice is of *great* value, and your service is great value. Know that before you go into *any* audition.

Auditions don't take that long for me anymore, and I do them all day long, in and out of the studio. I'm also spread across several P2Ps. I have eight different agents that bring in jobs, as well as a ton of repeat clients. Also, for such clients, some of *their* clients are new: they don't yet know my voice, and so my repeat client wants me to audition for their new client. I do a lot of those.

The bottom line is you are an *actor!* You *must* be willing to audition. That's how we get cast: by auditioning. It just makes sense. It's a numbers game. Your ability to audition and crank them out, and your willingness to do them repeatedly is going to be a huge determinant as far as whether or not you'll actually get cast, as well as how frequently. Beyond that, it's up to fate. Don't hang your hat on any one audition. Keep planting seeds.

One of my blogs I'd like to reference is "Stars, Listens & Likes Oh My!"[85] This blog is all about not steering your life by the rearview mirror. *Visit and read this blog.* Your eyes will be opened. Don't crave that validation and some kind of potential sign that you might get cast. The key word is *might*. So what? Keep moving! While you're sitting there biting your nails over it, others are getting in line in front of you for the next one, which pays more and might be right up your alley. Don't pin your hopes to any single audition. Your hopes will be dashed and your nails will be jagged.

You have to develop a love for auditions, and auditioning quickly. The moment you develop any kind of contempt for continuing to do auditions, or stepping back into the studio ("Ugh, I was *just* in there!") could be the beginning of the end for you.

This career is a very reactive, "drop everything" career; you must be willing to do an audition at the drop of a hat. You must be willing to surrender what you're doing and try out for that role, because that's how you get cast, and getting cast is how you get paid. Do you remember Bette Midler's character in *Beaches*? She was about to be married to Michael, the doctor...and she suddenly called it off. She was confronted by Barbara Hershey's character. Why did she call it off?

A lead. A lead role. A "chance to come back from the dead", as she called it. I'm not advocating breaking people's hearts and not fulfilling your vows. I *am* however advocating that you jump at each role as a "chance to come back from the dead": that space in between jobs where you're waiting. You *can* be alive in that space.

I GOT CAST! NOW WHAT???

Now let's talk about what happens *after* booking.

It's really important that you have contracts in place. Some of the P2Ps like Voices.com, The Voice Realm and Voiceovers.com have systems in place where they can book you directly through the P2P, and their money goes into Escrow. (I do *not* recommend you use The Voice Realm: again, please see my chapter on "2P or not 2P: That is the Question.") Voice123 has recently begun doing this, and allows it when the clients want to bill through their escrow, although the overwhelming majority of my jobs through Voice123 are direct-billed.

For independently billed jobs where the client is your direct client (and not the P2P's client), you're going to want to have documents in place that are ready to go: contracts with clauses that protect you and your interests. Have these prepared and in place *beforehand*, because when a client books, you have very little time to prepare a contract template and send it to them. They're usually wanting to get that recording going. Make them official, branded with your logo and contact information! You can visit www.supervoiceoverdocs.com: that is a website of mine that provides contract templates, marketing templates, stationery, letterhead examples, logo examples, email templates, a goal tracking worksheet, etc: several documents you're going to need to help you run a sound voiceover business. If you don't have the gumption or the wherewithal to develop your own contracts, there are templates available there.

Make sure and thank your client when you've been booked! Gratitude goes a *long* way! It makes the world go round. Thank a client *profusely* for hiring you. I am often criticized by my family for being a chronic over-thanker. I prefer this to the alternative!

Make sure and keep client emails to follow up with them. Some of the P2Ps will forbid you from having direct communication with your client, because you're circumventing their system. This is one of the reasons why I detest The Voice Realm. And you can get booted off TVR's site just for *asking* for someone's email, or for providing yours. You do have to be careful to observe any site's TOU of course, no matter how despicable they may be.

In any other matchmaking service like Voice123's, you can communicate directly with the client over email. Harvest that email, save it, put it in your CRM for holiday follow-ups, for updates, for discounts and specials, or for any news that you want to share with them.

Ever heard of SourceConnect, ISDN, or ipDTL? Be prepared for directed sessions! Clients will use these, as well as Skype, phone, Microsoft Teams, Freeconferencecall.com, Google Meet, Discord, Zoom, etc. Those are the new reality. You have to be prepared for those. Understand how they work, and do your due diligence. Figure out what you need to put in place: this functionality is actually a selling point with your audition, and it's something that you will want to include in your audition notes. "I am SourceConnect ready." That's music to the ears of some casting directors! They want someone who has SourceConnect. It's a wonderful feature that you can offer them.

And payment! Oh, that glorious word. The only thing I like better than sending a contract is sending an invoice. Truly! It's wonderful to know that your job is done, and now you can bill. Make sure your invoice reflects *exactly* what you told them they would receive, at exactly the same cost. Set yourself up as amenably as possible for every client in terms of payment avenues. Get many or all of the following accounts setup to receive payments, so a client can jump on any one of them that is most convenient for them. Some of these services are:

- Check or money order
- ACH (Automated Clearing House)
- Bill.com
- Paypal
- Veem
- Venmo
- Square
- Stripe
- Wise
- ChasePay
- Zelle
- Authorize.net
- Others

Receiving payments for your hard work – and it is hard! – as a voice talent, is a deeply rewarding feeling.

Remember, just like in the movie *Highlander*, there can be only *one*. This is an act of survival and success. Remember that every audition begets sometimes hundreds of auditioners, and there really truly can be only *one*. Are you that one?

Read the script. Read the casting specs, know that you have what it takes to deliver that script. Intend. Don't just hope; *intend*. Read it like you *believe* in it, and you'll get cast! Not every time, of course, but you'll get closer and closer to being cast a lot more frequently.

Just remember that if the script is something that you can deliver, and it's in your wheelhouse, then by all means try - and like Yoda said "*Try not. Do* - or do not. There is no try." Give it your all! Go into each audition committed to win.

At the beginning of 2021, after an especially brutal year in so many respects, a voiceover colleague said, "365 new days; 365 new chances." So true! Every audition and marketing outreach is a chance. Every single one is a golden opportunity for you to connect with a client… be awarded a script… be able to do what you love, which is voiceovers.

The auditions are out there in plenty, and you *can* do this: I mean that with every ounce of me.

CONCLUSION

THAT'S A WRAP!

Thank you so much for reading this. I pray you get vision and clarity for your voiceover endeavors. Terri Apple said: "Having a great voice isn't enough. Learning what to do with it is the key to a long and lucrative career."[86] Amen to that!

I hope and pray this book has been greatly illuminating, inspiring, and empowering for you as a budding or established voice talent. I've "been there, said that." Go there and say that too. Bill DeWees talks about his success frequently throughout his book, *How to Start and build a Six Figure Voice Over Business*: "I am not dreaming about being a big star, or getting well-known. I don't care about Academy Awards or any other awards, for that matter. I care about making as much money as possible in my voice over business and I do whatever it takes to make it happen."[87]

I agree! I almost scoff at the Voice Arts Awards (or SOVAS) because they're just not what I'm about. I'm not implying that they don't have value, they do to many! But I don't want or need such acclaim, statues, or fame. What would I do with a little golden statue anyway? Admire it for a few weeks and then put it up on a shelf and *maybe* notice it here and there? What I notice is getting repeatedly cast. I notice a new client adding me to their roster. I notice connections. I notice invoices paid. I just simply want to provide for my family doing something that I love. That's my aim, and I've accomplished it for several years now.

I don't do anything else now except voiceovers. I provide them full-time, and I am currently poised for a third of a million dollars in income in 2021 just from voiceovers. That's a drastic improvement over 2020. Will I get there? We'll see. But goals are in place to do it, as they should be.

I have an innate sense of hustle and *drive* that cannot be extinguished easily, save by staying up late because of my two boys, and then desperately craving sleep the following day. I am *pulled* back into my studio to get work done. It's gravitational. It is my *pleasure*, my *joy*, and I *love* what I do. That pull drives me to succeed. I love to work hard and smart, and I love to give of my knowledge of how I do so. I hope you have received just a smidge of that through this book.

Remember again what Thibaut said: success is not an event. It's a *journey*. My plan is to stay on that road. May it never end.

I want to be a tremendous part of your success. That's why I wrote this book: to pay homage to those who have been a great part of my success, and to edify them, but also to encourage you that you *too* can continue the legacy of success and far exceed what I and so many others have been able to accomplish in this business called voiceovers.

May all your dreams come true in this endeavor, and may God bless you. #youcandothis

We are superheroes, us voice talent. This theme is prevalent all throughout my books, *The Super Voiceover Artist Book Series* at supervoiceoverbook.com.

If you are an actor, particularly a voice actor, you are made of some pretty *stern* stuff. You are *resilient*. You have *tenacity*. You face rejection and insurmountable odds every single day. And yet, you somehow rise again, and stand tall above the smoking rubble around you. You dust yourself off, and soar into the heavens yet again. You steel yourself for the auditions you face, and give them your all, because one thing is true: You are a *warrior*. You are a *dynamo*. You, my good voiceover friend, are a *freaking superhero*. May you be awarded jobs faster than a speeding bullet. Thank you for being in this battle with me, saving the world…one voiceover at a time.

I cannot freaking believe I get to do this every day, and I have the utmost confidence that you can do it too. I believe in you. It's no mistake that the word "can" is in this book 275 times (now 276). It's because you truly CAN do this. (277).

This concludes our bioanecstruction lesson for the day. There is *so* much more that I could say, and there is *so* much more that you and I both can learn. The voiceover industry is changing and evolving all of the time. Running a business demands that you stay flexible, be willing to adopt new tools, and try out new avenues of marketing and outreach. It's all a giant maze, and a rolling stone gathers no moss. So…keep rolling.

Additionally, my way is not the only way. There are many, many paths to success, as long as you remember to treat it respectfully as a *business*. I hope that what I offered you in this book opens your eyes to the fact that you *are* more than able to do this as a successful business for yourself.

I am nothing special, just a little fish in a big pond, who decided to swim one way with all his might. If I can do it, so can you.

Go git 'em.

Joshua Alexander

ABOUT THE AUTHOR

JOSHUA ALEXANDER: VOICEOVER ARTIST · AUTHOR · BLOGGER

Joshua is a man who takes his business seriously, but doesn't take *himself* too seriously. This voice talent extraordinaire is no hassle, with under an hour usual turnaround time depending on length of script. Joshua has excellent pricing. He has broadcast-level home studio quality, and experience with roots back in 1993. His artist roots began at a marketing company in Seattle, where he sold PSA's to businesses, and voiced many of those spots on the radio. He said "this is pretty cool," and the rest was history.

Joshua is a former traveling Christian singer / speaker / performer, and has received airplay on KCMS 105.3FM in Seattle. He's done jingles too! He loves his wife and two boys, and loves Jesus. He lives a life of deep gratitude and joy, because he's content and found his calling. Oh yeah...and he's deathly afraid of spiders. No really. Deathly. Don't judge him.

Joshua has done radio broadcasting, PSA's, and video production incorporating voice-acting work in a career serving clients all over the world. He has a storied career from the comfort of his home, and he loves what he does.

He's been interviewed countless times by podcasters and show hosts, and has been a featured speaker at major international conferences such as *OneVoice*[88] and the Latino conference *VoiceMasters*.[89] He's taught at several workshops on marketing, business operations, auditions, the P2P's, and more.

Joshua gives back heavily to the voiceover community. He recognizes he's been given a lot, so he pays it forward through free 20-minute voiceover video consults via posts on Reddit, where he advises on next steps for newbies and how to ramp up one's game for the veterans. He answers voiceover questions on Quora. He provides demo critiques as well. Joshua longs to be a strong part of the voiceover community at large: sharing, imparting, teaching, and encouraging others about the value of running a voiceover business, and not a hobby.

Joshua maintains The Voices In My Head Blog[90], a blog with a growing subscriber base meant to encourage and inspire through laughter.

On Mondays at 1pm PST, Joshua runs "VoiceOverdrive", a weekly transparent report on voiceovers meant to encourage and show that a full-time career in voiceovers truly is possible, through his Instagram channel, @seattlevoiceoverartist[91]. He also is a frequent poster of encouraging videos meant to rev up the VO industry.

Joshua also facilitates The Global Voiceover Artists Network on Facebook[92], a growing community of like-minded aspiring and veteran voice talent, and ran the North Seattle & Everett Voiceover Meetup group which met monthly from 2017 to 2019 and hosted featured speakers and workshops.

In addition to providing voiceover services and blogging about voiceovers, Joshua has self-produced a robust voiceover business training program entitled "The Super Voiceover Business Video Package." It's available at supervoiceovertraining.com. Comprised of 12 modules spanning over two hours of incredibly in-depth content, Joshua delivers in an unscripted, highly conversational teaching style. It's connective and encouraging, loaded with business insight spanning three decades in voiceovers and two in entrepreneurship. Check it out today!

Joshua lives in Washington with his wife, Janine, sons Brennan and Asher, Macy the dog, and Winston the cat. And due to having kids, goldfish are most likely in the future. But due to having a cat, they may soon be in the past. Please check back for updates.

On that note, check out all three books of Joshua's books in the "Super Voiceover Artist" book trilogy at supervoiceoverbook.com.

Representation provided by:

Colleen Bell Talent Agency
Lori Lins Ltd
Impressive Talent

The Sheppard Agency
AB2 Talent

Contact Joshua via:

Email: josh@supervoiceover.com
Website: www.supervoiceover.com
Facebook: www.joshyface.com
Instagram: www.joshygram.com
Pinterest: www.joshypin.com
LinkedIn: www.joshylinked.com
Twitter: www.joshytweet.com
YouTube: www.joshyvids.com

RECOMMENDED READING

I highly recommend the following books and resources for your voiceover pursuit, business, or career:

Making Money in your PJs: Freelancing for Voice Actors and other Solopreneurs by Paul Strikwerda

V-Oh! Tip, Tricks, Tools and Techniques to Start and Sustain Your Voiceover Career by Marc Cashman

The Voiceover Startup Guide: How to Land Your First VO Job by Chris Agos

There's Money Where Your Mouth Is by Elaine A Clark

Voiceover Achiever by Celia Siegel

How to Start and Build a SIX FIGURE VoiceOver Business: Set Your VO Career on Fire! by Bill DeWees

The E-Myth by Michael Gerber

Voice Over Man by Peter Dickson

BIBLIOGRAPHY

[1] en.wikipedia.org/wiki/Kobayashi_Maru
[2] *Making Money in your PJs: Freelancing for voice-overs and other solopreneurs*, Paul Strikwerda, 2014 edition, page 369-370
[3] wp.nyu.edu/dispatch/2020/03/20/voice-over-trends-in-2020-and-why-voice-over-coaching-remains-more-important-than-ever/
[4] ibid
[5] www.facebook.com/groups/votechtalk/
[6] www.facebook.com/groups/VOPeeps/
[7] www.facebook.com/groups/globalvoiceovertalent/
[8] www.supervoiceover.com/2p-or-not-2p-that-is-the-question/
[9] www.youtube.com/channel/UCHHf1h8k7MA6-AG8FXjnQSw
[10] www.jordanaudio.ninja/
[11] www.vobs.tv/
[12] votechguru.com/
[13] www.antlandproductions.com/Voice-Overs.html
[14] www.nethervoice.com/shop
[15] www.amazon.com/Voice-Over-Voice-Actor-Yuri-Lowenthal/dp/0984074058
[16] www.amazon.com/V-Oh-Tricks-Techniques-Sustain-Voiceover/dp/0990395804
[17] www.amazon.com/Art-Voice-Acting-Performing-Voiceover/dp/0415736978
[18] www.amazon.com/Start-Build-FIGURE-Business-Career-ebook/dp/B00A2E7NCC
[19] www.amazon.com/Voice-Over-Startup-Guide-Acting/dp/0982886365
[20] www.amazon.com/Voiceover-Man-Extraordinary-Story-Professional-ebook/dp/B08HN3TFRF
[21] www.amazon.com/Voiceover-Achiever-Brand-career-Change/dp/0692991808
[22] www.supervoiceoverbook.com
[23] supervoiceover.com/teaching/
[24] iwanttobeavoiceactor.com/
[25] *Making Money in your PJs: Freelancing for voice-overs and other solopreneurs*, Paul Strikwerda, 2014 edition, page 63
[26] www.backstage.com/magazine/article/essentials-every-vo-audition-9190/
[27] *How to Start and Build a Six Figure Voice Over Business*, Bill DeWees, 2013 edition, page 47
[28] www-users.cs.york.ac.uk/susan/joke/essay.htm
[29] www.foresthillretirement.org/stress-reducing-hobbies/
[30] *There's Money Where Your Mouth Is*, Elaine Clark, Fourth Edition, page 290
[31] www.voicezam.com/
[32] www.voiceactorwebsites.com
[33] ctworkerscompattorney.com/
[34] www.supervoiceoverdocs.com
[35] www.uptimerobot.com
[36] supervoiceover.com/i-am-a-voice-talent-and-i-wear-makeup/
[37] www.globalvoiceacademy.com/gvaa-rate-guide-2/
[38] voiceovers.com/vo/rates
[39] www.voicezam.com
[40] fractalfoundation.org/resources/what-is-chaos-theory/
[41] *Making Money in your PJ's: Freelancing for voice-overs and other solopreneurs*, Paul Strikwerda, 2014 edition, page 23
[42] www.dalecarnegie.com/en/courses/3741
[43] www.amazon.com/Upgrade-Yourself-Strategies-Transform-Mindset-ebook/dp/B079VN6HK9
[44] *Making Money in your PJs: Freelancing for voice-overs and other solopreneurs*, Paul Strikwerda, 2014 edition, page 325
[45] *Voice-Over Voice Actor:* 2018, Yuri Lowenthal & Tara Platt, page 185
[46] ibid, page 166
[47] www.supervoiceover.com/no-thanks-i-already-know-everything/
[48] www.linkedin.com/pulse/networking-collecting-contacts-planting-relations-misha-griffiths/
[49] www.facebook.com/themiccheckvoworkout

[50] www.patfraley.com/pf/
[51] www.fixinthemix.com/
[52] www.elaineclarkvo.com/
[53] www.jmcvoiceover.com
[54] www.voiceactingdirector.com/
[55] www.kaybess.com/vocoaching/
[56] www.antlandproductions.com/Voice-Overs.html
[57] www.cashmancommercials.com/
[58] www.davefennoy.com/studyvo/
[59] podcasts.apple.com/us/podcast/the-voiceover-insider-podcast/id944751635
[60] www.bobbergen.com/voclass.htm
[61] www.anneganguzza.com/voiceover-coaching
[62] www.juliewilliamscoaches.com/about/
[63] myemail.constantcontact.com/Buy-Recording---Building-Your-VO-Business-For-Tomorrow--with-J--Michael-Collins-.html
[64] www.nrtw.org
[65] www.tomdheere.com/voiceovers-voice-bank-and-voices-dot-com-the-not-silent-blog-81517/
[66] www.voiceoverxtra.com/article.htm?id=JLC54R2O
[67] www.toddschick.com/voices-com-review/
[68] www.voices.com/company/press/2019/partnership-with-vocalid
[69] globalvoiceacademy.com/gvaa-rate-guide-2/
[70] rates.gravyforthebrain.com/
[71] voiceovers.com/vo/rates
[72] *Making Money in your PJs: Freelancing for voice-overs and other solopreneurs*, Paul Strikwerda, 2014 edition, page 308
[73] ibid, page 316
[74] *Making Money in your PJs: Freelancing for voice-overs and other solopreneurs*, Paul Strikwerda, 2014 edition, page 320
[75] *There's Money Where Your Mouth Is*, Elaine Clark, Fourth Edition, page 204
[76] www.gvoa.net/
[77] tomdheere.com/voiceovers-tension-08-06-19
[78] www.voice123.com/blog/voice123/the-voice-acting-payment-riddle-and-how-to-solve-it/
[79] www.jmcvoiceover.com/2018/12/12/updates-from-voice123-regarding-the-new-site/
[80] en.wikipedia.org/wiki/UK_miners%27_strike_(1984%E2%80%9385)
[81] supervoiceover.com/how-do-i-get-started-in-voiceovers/
[82] www.backstage.com/magazine/article/essentials-every-vo-audition-9190/
[83] *How to Start and Build a Six Figure Voice Over Business*, Bill DeWees, 2013 edition, page 47
[84] *Voice-Over Voice Actor: 2018*, Yuri Lowenthal & Tara Platt, page 88
[85] www.supervoiceover.com/stars-listens-likes-oh-my/
[86] *Making Money in Voice-Overs,* Terri Apple, Lone Eagle Publishing Company (1999)
[87] *How to Start and Build a Six Figure Voice Over Business*, Bill DeWees, 2013 edition, page 105
[88] www.onevoiceconference.com/
[89] www.congresodelavoz.com/congreso-de-la-voz-online-2020/
[90] www.itsthevoicesinmyhead.com
[91] www.joshygram.com
[92] www.gvoa.net